Buzzing Beginnings: A Beginner's Guide to Beekeeping

A Handbook to Apiculture

Table of Contents

Copyright © 2023 David Meyer

All rights reserved. No part of this book may be reproduced

or used in any manner without the prior written permission of the copyright owner,

except for the use of brief quotations in a book review.

To request permissions, contact the publisher at dntmeyerllc@gmail.com

Table Of Contents

Chapter 1: Introduction to Beekeeping

A. What is beekeeping?

B. Benefits of beekeeping

C. Understanding the importance of bees in the ecosystem

Chapter 2: Getting Started

A. Research and education

1. Joining local beekeeping associations or clubs

2. Reading books, online resources, and attending workshops

B. Legal considerations and regulations

1. Checking local ordinances and zoning restrictions

2. Registering your beehives, if required

Chapter 3: Essential Equipment and Tools

A. Beehive components

1. Hive bodies (boxes)

2. Frames and foundation

3. Inner and outer covers

B. Protective clothing and gear

1. Bee suit or jacket

2. Veil and gloves

3. Smoker and hive tool

C. Additional tools and supplies

1. Bee brush

2. Honey extractor

3. Feeder and water source

Chapter 4: Selecting Honey Bee Species

A. Common honey bee species

B. Factors to consider when choosing a species

1. Climate suitability

2. Temperament and behavior

3. Disease resistance

Chapter 5: Choosing a Suitable Location

A. Considerations for hive placement

1. Access to sunlight

2. Protection from strong winds

3. Distance from neighbors and public areas

B. Providing a water source

C. Ensuring forage availability

Chapter 6: Installing and Managing Bees

A. Acquiring bees

1. Purchasing packages or nucs (nucleus colonies)

2. Capturing swarms or performing hive splits

B. Installing bees in the hive

C. Regular hive inspections and maintenance

1. Checking for signs of disease and pests

2. Managing honey production and hive expansion

D. Feeding bees, if necessary

Chapter 7: Beekeeping Challenges and Solutions

A. Common problems and pests

1. Varroa mites and other parasites

2. Diseases and infections

B. Swarm prevention and management

C. Honey harvesting and processing

D. Winter preparation and hive survival

Chapter 8: Safety and Health Considerations

A. Understanding bee stings and allergic reactions

B. Proper handling techniques to minimize stings

C. Using protective gear and maintaining hygiene

D. Seeking medical attention, if necessary

Chapter 9: Connecting with the Beekeeping Community

A. Participating in local beekeeping events

B. Networking with experienced beekeepers

C. Sharing knowledge and experiences

Chapter 1
Introduction

to Beekeeping

What is beekeeping?

Beekeeping, also known as apiculture, is the practice of maintaining and managing bee colonies, usually in hives, to collect honey, beeswax, and other bee-related products. Beekeepers, also called apiarists, engage in beekeeping as a hobby or as a commercial venture.

Honey production: Honey is the most well-known product of beekeeping. Beekeepers provide suitable habitats for bees, such as beehives, and take care of the colonies to encourage honey production. They harvest the excess honey while leaving enough for the bees' sustenance.

Pollination services: Bees play a crucial role in pollination, aiding the reproduction of many plants. Commercial beekeepers often provide pollination services to farmers by renting out their hives to be placed in orchards, fields, or greenhouses during the flowering season. The bees pollinate the crops, enhancing their yield and quality.

Beeswax production: Beeswax is a natural substance secreted by bees to build their honeycombs. Beekeepers collect beeswax, which has various applications, including candle making, cosmetics, and pharmaceuticals.

Hive management: Beekeepers ensure the health and well-being of the bee colonies. This includes inspecting the hives regularly, checking for signs of disease or parasites, providing suitable food sources, and maintaining the hive structure.

Swarm prevention and control: Bees have a natural tendency to reproduce by swarming, where a portion of the colony leaves with a new queen to establish a new hive. Beekeepers take measures to prevent swarming or capture and relocate swarms to prevent loss of bees.

Harvesting honey and other products: Beekeepers collect honeycomb frames, extract the honey using specialized equipment, and process it for consumption or sale. They may also collect beeswax, propolis, and royal jelly.

Beekeeping requires knowledge of bee behavior, hive management techniques, and understanding of the seasonal cycles and needs of the bees. It is essential to prioritize the health and welfare of the bees to maintain sustainable and productive colonies. Many beekeepers also contribute to conservation efforts by providing habitat for bees and promoting pollinator-friendly practices in their communities.

Benefits of beekeeping

Beekeeping offers a range of benefits, both for beekeepers and the broader environment.

Honey production: Beekeeping provides a source of delicious, natural honey. Honey is not only a sweetener but also has numerous health benefits. It contains antioxidants, enzymes, vitamins, and minerals, and has been used for its medicinal properties for centuries.

Pollination: Bees are vital pollinators, and beekeeping supports the pollination of many plants, including agricultural crops, fruits, vegetables, and flowers. By keeping bees, beekeepers help ensure the reproduction and yield of these plants, contributing to food production and ecosystem health.

Biodiversity and ecosystem support: Beekeeping promotes biodiversity by providing habitats for bees and other pollinators. It helps maintain and preserve native bee populations, which are crucial for the diversity and stability of ecosystems.

Crop production and quality: Many crops depend on bees for efficient pollination, leading to higher yields and better-quality produce. Beekeeping services, where hives are rented out for pollination, are widely utilized in agriculture to enhance crop productivity.

Education and awareness: Beekeeping provides an opportunity for education and raising awareness about the importance of bees and their role in the environment. Beekeepers often engage in outreach activities, such as school visits or public demonstrations, to share knowledge about bees and promote environmental conservation.

Sustainable agriculture: Beekeeping is aligned with sustainable agricultural practices. By promoting natural pollination, it reduces the reliance on chemical fertilizers and pesticides. Additionally, beekeepers often adopt organic or bee-friendly farming methods to protect the health of their bees and maintain a healthy ecosystem.

Products beyond honey: Beekeeping yields products beyond honey, such as beeswax, propolis, royal jelly, and pollen. These products have various applications in cosmetics, pharmaceuticals, candles, and dietary supplements, contributing to local economies and industries.

Personal satisfaction and hobby: Beekeeping can be a fulfilling hobby or a small-scale business venture. It allows individuals to connect with nature, learn about bee behavior, and enjoy the rewards of harvesting honey and other bee-related products.

Understanding the importance of bees in the ecosystem

Bees play a vital role in maintaining ecosystem health and functioning.

Pollination: Bees are one of the most effective pollinators in nature. They transfer pollen from the male parts (anthers) of flowers to the female parts (stigma), facilitating fertilization and seed production. Approximately 75% of the world's leading food crops depend on animal pollination, and bees are responsible for pollinating a significant portion of them. Fruits, vegetables, nuts, and oilseeds are heavily reliant on bee pollination, contributing to food security and agricultural productivity.

Biodiversity and Habitat Support: Bees are essential for maintaining biodiversity. They contribute to the reproduction of numerous plant species, including many wildflowers. By pollinating a wide range of plants, bees promote genetic diversity and the survival of various ecosystems. Bees and their diverse habitats also support other wildlife, such as birds and insects, creating a balanced and thriving ecosystem.

Wildflower and Forest Regeneration: Bees play a crucial role in the regeneration of wildflowers and forests. They help plants reproduce by pollinating both wildflowers in natural habitats and trees in forests. This process allows for the growth of new plants and ensures the continuation of diverse plant communities.

Seed Dispersal: Certain bee species are capable of collecting and transporting seeds. They gather pollen on their bodies while foraging and inadvertently spread pollen to other flowers, aiding in seed dispersal and plant colonization in new areas.

Ecosystem Services: Bees provide valuable ecosystem services beyond pollination. Through their foraging activities, bees contribute to nutrient cycling, soil fertility, and the maintenance of plant communities. They also support the survival of other pollinators by providing floral resources and habitat.

Food Web Support: Bees are part of intricate food webs, serving as a food source for various predators and contributing to the overall biodiversity of the ecosystem. They are preyed upon by birds, mammals, reptiles, amphibians, and other insects.

Environmental Indicators: Bees are sensitive to changes in their environment, including pollution, habitat loss, and climate change. Monitoring bee populations can provide valuable insights into the overall health of ecosystems. Declines in bee populations can signal environmental disturbances and imbalances that may have far-reaching effects on ecosystems and human well-being.

It is important to recognize the significance of bees in maintaining ecological balance and take measures to protect and conserve their populations and habitats. This includes promoting pollinator-friendly practices, reducing pesticide use, preserving natural habitats, and supporting initiatives that prioritize bee health and sustainability.

Chapter 2.

Getting Started

Research and education

Research and education are fundamental pillars for advancing knowledge and understanding in any field, including beekeeping.

Scientific advancements: Research in beekeeping leads to discoveries and advancements in various aspects of bee biology, hive management, disease prevention, and sustainable practices. It contributes to developing evidence-based guidelines and techniques that improve beekeeping methods, bee health, and honey production.

Understanding bee behavior and biology: Research helps us better understand the behavior, physiology, and life cycle of bees. This knowledge is essential for effective hive management, disease prevention, and addressing environmental challenges. It enables beekeepers to provide suitable conditions for their colonies and make informed decisions regarding beekeeping practices.

Disease prevention and management: Research plays a critical role in identifying and understanding bee diseases, parasites, and pests. Through scientific investigations, new strategies for disease prevention, control, and treatment can be developed. This helps beekeepers in managing and mitigating the impact of diseases, ultimately leading to healthier and more productive colonies.

Sustainable practices: Research promotes the development and adoption of sustainable beekeeping practices. It focuses on minimizing the use of chemical treatments, promoting natural pest and disease control methods, and reducing environmental impacts. Sustainable practices help maintain bee health, preserve biodiversity, and safeguard the long-term viability of beekeeping as an industry.

Conservation and habitat preservation: Research informs efforts to conserve wild bee populations and their habitats. It helps identify the factors contributing to the decline of wild bees and guides conservation strategies. Understanding the ecological relationships between bees and their environment is crucial for effective habitat preservation and restoration.

Education and training: Education is vital for both novice and experienced beekeepers. Formal and informal educational programs provide the necessary knowledge and skills to engage in successful beekeeping practices. Workshops, courses, and training sessions conducted by experts and experienced beekeepers enable beekeepers to learn new techniques, exchange ideas, and stay updated with the latest developments in the field.

Awareness and public outreach: Research and education play a role in raising public awareness about the importance of bees and their conservation. They help disseminate knowledge about the vital role bees play in pollination, food production, and ecosystem health. By increasing public understanding, research and education efforts can garner support for bee-friendly initiatives, policies, and habitat preservation.

Research and education are ongoing processes that contribute to the continuous improvement and sustainability of beekeeping practices. They provide the foundation for beekeepers to make informed decisions, protect bee health, and contribute to the conservation of bees and their ecosystems.

Joining local beekeeping associations or clubs

Joining local beekeeping associations or clubs can be highly beneficial for both novice and experienced beekeepers.

Knowledge sharing: Beekeeping associations and clubs bring together beekeepers with different levels of experience and expertise. By joining, you can tap into a wealth of knowledge and learn from experienced beekeepers. They often organize educational programs, workshops, and seminars on beekeeping techniques, hive management, disease prevention, and other relevant topics. This exchange of knowledge can enhance your skills and understanding of beekeeping.

Networking and community: Beekeeping associations provide a platform to connect with like-minded individuals who share a passion for beekeeping. You can meet fellow beekeepers, exchange ideas, discuss challenges, and share successes. Being part of a community of beekeepers can be inspiring, supportive, and motivating, particularly when facing specific beekeeping issues or seeking advice.

Mentorship opportunities: Many associations offer mentorship programs where experienced beekeepers mentor newcomers. Having a mentor can be invaluable as they can guide you through the practical aspects of beekeeping, provide personalized advice, and help you navigate challenges specific to your local area.

Access to resources and equipment: Beekeeping associations often have shared resources, such as libraries with books and publications on beekeeping. Some associations may also have equipment lending programs, enabling you to borrow or rent specialized beekeeping equipment before making significant investments.

Legislative and regulatory updates: Beekeeping associations can keep you informed about local regulations, permits, and best practices related to beekeeping. They may advocate for beekeeping-friendly policies and provide guidance on compliance with local laws, ensuring that your beekeeping activities align with legal requirements.

Bee health initiatives: Associations often play an active role in promoting bee health and conservation efforts. They may organize initiatives for disease monitoring, pest control, and sustainable beekeeping practices. By joining, you can contribute to these initiatives and participate in collective efforts to protect and preserve bee populations.

Beekeeping events and exhibitions: Many associations organize beekeeping events, fairs, conferences, or exhibitions where beekeepers can showcase their products, exchange ideas, and stay up-to-date with the latest trends and innovations in beekeeping.

To find a local beekeeping association or club, you can search online, check with agricultural extension offices, contact local beekeepers, or inquire at nearby agricultural supply stores. Being an active member of such an organization can provide valuable support, resources, and a sense of camaraderie as you embark on your beekeeping journey.

Reading books, online resources, and attending workshops

Engaging in various educational resources and attending workshops are excellent ways to enhance your knowledge and skills in beekeeping. Here are some benefits of reading books, exploring online resources, and attending workshops.

Comprehensive knowledge: Books dedicated to beekeeping provide in-depth information on various aspects, including bee biology, hive management techniques, disease prevention, and honey production. They offer a structured and comprehensive learning experience, allowing you to gain a solid foundation in beekeeping principles.

Diverse perspectives: Books written by different authors or experts can present a range of perspectives and approaches to beekeeping. This exposure to various viewpoints can broaden your understanding and enable you to make informed decisions based on a broader knowledge base.

Detailed guidance: Books often provide step-by-step instructions, illustrations, and practical tips for beekeeping tasks. They can guide you through specific processes, such as hive construction, honey extraction, or queen rearing, with detailed explanations that allow you to follow along effectively.

Online resources and forums: The internet offers a wealth of information on beekeeping. Websites, blogs, and forums dedicated to beekeeping provide a platform for sharing experiences, asking questions, and learning from other beekeepers worldwide. You can find instructional videos, articles, and discussion threads that address specific beekeeping topics and challenges.

Real-time updates: Online resources are frequently updated with the latest advancements, research findings, and best practices in beekeeping. Staying connected to online platforms ensures you have access to up-to-date information and emerging trends in the field.

Interactive learning: Workshops and training programs provide hands-on experience and practical demonstrations. Attending workshops led by experienced beekeepers allows you to observe techniques firsthand, ask questions, and receive immediate feedback. These interactive sessions can enhance your understanding and confidence in beekeeping practices.

Networking opportunities: Workshops and training events bring together beekeepers from various backgrounds and experience levels. Networking with other participants and instructors can lead to valuable connections, mentorship opportunities, and ongoing support throughout your beekeeping journey.

Access to specialized topics: Books, online resources, and workshops often cover specialized topics within beekeeping, such as queen rearing, honeybee genetics, or integrated pest management. Engaging with these resources allows you to delve deeper into specific areas of interest and expand your expertise in those areas.

When utilizing online resources, it's important to ensure they come from reputable sources, such as established beekeeping organizations, academic institutions, or experienced beekeepers. Verifying the credibility of the information and cross-referencing multiple sources can help ensure accurate and reliable information.

Combining books, online resources, and workshops offers a well-rounded approach to learning beekeeping, allowing you to acquire knowledge, gain practical skills, and stay updated on the latest developments in the field.

Legal considerations and regulations

Legal considerations and regulations play a crucial role in beekeeping to ensure the well-being of bees, protect the environment, and address potential risks. Here are some key aspects of legal considerations and regulations in beekeeping:

Registration and permits: In some regions, beekeepers may be required to register their hives or obtain permits before engaging in beekeeping activities. This helps regulatory authorities track beekeeping operations, monitor bee health, and enforce compliance with relevant regulations.

Zoning and land use regulations: Local zoning and land use regulations may specify where beekeeping is permitted and under what conditions. These regulations may determine the allowable number of hives, setback distances from property lines or public spaces, and any restrictions on hive placement. It is important to consult local authorities or agricultural extension offices to understand and comply with the specific regulations in your area.

Apiary location and hive density: Some regulations may govern the proximity of hives to residential areas, public spaces, or sensitive locations. These regulations aim to prevent conflicts with neighbors, ensure public safety, and protect sensitive populations, such as individuals with allergies to bee stings.

Disease management and biosecurity: Regulations may address disease management and biosecurity measures to prevent the spread of bee diseases and pests. Beekeepers may be required to follow specific protocols for disease prevention, hive inspections, and reporting of any suspected or diagnosed diseases.

Pesticide use and application: Regulations often exist to govern the use and application of pesticides, as certain pesticides can be harmful to bees. Beekeepers may need to adhere to specific guidelines regarding the timing of pesticide application, bee forage protection, and the use of bee-safe pesticides.

Transportation and movement of bees: When transporting bees for pollination services or other purposes, regulations may require permits, health certifications, or specific procedures to prevent the spread of diseases and pests. This helps protect local bee populations and mitigate risks associated with long-distance bee movement.

Labeling and honey standards: Regulations may establish standards for honey labeling, ensuring accurate information for consumers. These standards may include requirements for labeling honey origins, quality grades, and the disclosure of any additives or processing methods used.

Environmental considerations: Regulations may address environmental concerns related to beekeeping practices. This may include restrictions on the use of certain hive treatments or management practices that can have detrimental effects on water quality, wildlife, or native plant populations.

It's crucial for beekeepers to familiarize themselves with the specific legal requirements and regulations in their area. Consult local beekeeping associations, agricultural extension offices, or regulatory authorities to ensure compliance with applicable laws and regulations. By adhering to these legal considerations, beekeepers can contribute to responsible beekeeping practices and promote the well-being of bees and the environment.

Checking local ordinances and zoning restrictions

Checking local ordinances and zoning restrictions is an important step for beekeepers to ensure compliance with regulations specific to their area.

Research local ordinances: Start by researching local ordinances and regulations related to beekeeping. Contact your local city or town hall, municipal government, or agricultural extension office to inquire about any specific rules or permits related to beekeeping. They can provide you with information on zoning restrictions, hive placement guidelines, and any other relevant regulations that apply to your area.

Check zoning regulations: Zoning regulations determine land use and can impact whether beekeeping is allowed in certain areas or under certain conditions. Review the zoning ordinances specific to your property or intended beekeeping location. Look for any language related to beekeeping, agricultural activities, or animal husbandry. Note any restrictions or requirements, such as setback distances from property lines or restrictions on hive density.

Seek clarification: If the information you find is unclear or if you have specific questions, reach out to local officials or regulatory authorities responsible for enforcing zoning and land use regulations. They can provide further guidance and clarification on what is allowed and any specific restrictions or conditions that apply to beekeeping in your area.

Join local beekeeping associations: Local beekeeping associations or clubs often have members who are well-versed in local regulations and can provide insights and guidance based on their own experiences. They may have already navigated the local regulatory landscape and can share their knowledge with you.

Obtain necessary permits: If permits are required for beekeeping in your area, make sure to follow the necessary procedures to obtain them. This may involve filling out an application, paying fees, and meeting specific requirements set by local authorities. Adhering to the permit process ensures that you are operating within the legal framework and can avoid potential penalties or conflicts.

Remember that regulations can vary significantly from one location to another, so it's essential to research the specific ordinances and regulations that apply to your area. By understanding and complying with local ordinances and zoning restrictions, you can engage in beekeeping activities in a responsible and lawful manner.

Registering your beehives, if required

Registering your beehives, if required by local regulations, is an important step to ensure compliance with beekeeping laws and to support efforts in bee health monitoring and disease control.

Research local requirements: Start by researching the specific registration requirements for beekeeping in your area. Check with your local agricultural extension office, beekeeping associations, or regulatory authorities to understand if hive registration is mandatory and what the process entails.

Complete registration forms: If registration is required, you will likely need to fill out registration forms provided by the relevant authority. These forms typically ask for basic information about your apiary, such as the number of hives, their locations, your contact information, and other details they may require for record-keeping purposes.

Provide necessary documentation: Some registration processes may require additional documentation. This could include proof of property ownership or permission to keep bees on the property, proof of liability insurance, or health certificates for your bees. Make sure to gather any required documentation in advance to ensure a smooth registration process.

Submit registration forms: Once you have completed the registration forms and assembled any necessary documentation, submit them to the appropriate authority as specified in the registration guidelines. This may involve mailing the forms, submitting them online, or visiting a local office in person. Follow the instructions provided by the regulatory authority to ensure proper submission.

Pay registration fees: Depending on the location and specific regulations, there may be registration fees associated with registering your beehives. Ensure that you include any required fees along with your registration forms, following the payment instructions provided by the authority.

Renew registration as required: Some areas may require annual or periodic renewal of beehive registration. Stay informed about renewal requirements and make sure to submit any necessary renewal forms or fees within the specified timeframe.

Keep registration documentation accessible: Once you have successfully registered your beehives, keep your registration documentation readily available. This may include copies of registration forms, permits, or any other relevant paperwork. Having this documentation easily accessible can help demonstrate your compliance with local regulations if requested by authorities or in case of any inspections or inquiries.

Remember, registration requirements and processes can vary from one jurisdiction to another, so it's important to understand and follow the specific guidelines set by your local regulatory authority. By registering your beehives, you contribute to the responsible management of beekeeping activities and support initiatives aimed at monitoring bee health and disease prevention.

Chapter 3. Essential Equipment and Tools

Beehive components

Beehives consist of several components that provide shelter, support, and functionality for honeybees.

Bottom Board: The bottom board is the base of the beehive, serving as the foundation and providing an entrance and exit for the bees. It helps maintain ventilation and regulates the temperature within the hive.

Hive Bodies or Brood Boxes: Hive bodies, also known as brood boxes, are the main living space for the honeybees. They are typically rectangular boxes that contain frames for the bees to build, comb and raise broods. Hive bodies are where the queen lays eggs, and they serve as the primary storage area for pollen and honey.

Frames: Frames are wooden or plastic structures that hang inside the hive bodies and provide support for beeswax comb construction. They consist of a wooden frame with a removable foundation or sheet that the bees use to build their comb. Frames can be removed for inspection and honey extraction.

Supers: Supers are additional boxes placed on top of the hive bodies. They are used for honey storage, and honey supers typically contain frames with foundation or pre-drawn comb for the bees to fill with honey. Supers are added when there is sufficient nectar flow for the bees to produce surplus honey.

Inner Cover: The inner cover sits on top of the hive bodies or supers and provides insulation and ventilation. It has a small hole or notch that serves as an additional entrance and exit for the bees. The inner cover helps regulate temperature and humidity within the hive.

Outer Cover or Telescoping Cover: The outer cover, also known as a telescoping cover, is the topmost component of the hive. It provides protection from the elements and helps insulate the hive. The outer cover typically extends slightly beyond the edges of the hive to provide overhang and protect the hive from rain and snow.

Queen Excluder: A queen excluder is a wire or plastic grid placed between the brood boxes and supers. It has openings that allow worker bees to pass through but restrict the queen's access to the honey supers. This helps prevent the queen from laying eggs in the honey supers, keeping them free of brood.

These components work together to provide the honey bees with a suitable habitat for brood rearing, honey production, and overall colony health. Beekeepers can customize their hive setup based on their preferences and management practices, but the basic components described above form the foundation of a beehive.

Hive bodies (boxes)

Hive bodies, also known as boxes or brood boxes, are the main living space for honey bees within a beehive. They provide the bees with an area to raise broods and store pollen and honey.

Purpose: Hive bodies serve as the primary area where the queen bee lays her eggs and the brood develops. They provide the necessary space and resources for the growth and development of the honeybee colony.

Construction: Hive bodies are typically rectangular boxes made of wood, although some beekeepers may use alternative materials such as plastic or polystyrene. The dimensions of hive bodies can vary, but the most common size is the Langstroth hive body, which is approximately 20 inches long, 16 inches wide, and 9 5/8 inches deep.

Frames: Hive bodies contain frames, which are wooden or plastic structures that hang inside the box. Frames provide support for beeswax comb construction and serve as a foundation for the bees to build their cells. Each frame holds a removable foundation or sheet that guides the bees in constructing uniform comb.

Brood Rearing: The brood nest, located within the hive bodies, is where the queen lays her eggs. The worker bees care for the brood and maintain the optimal temperature for their development. The brood includes eggs, larvae, and capped brood.

Storage Space: Hive bodies also offer space for storing pollen and honey. Pollen is collected by worker bees as a protein source, while honey serves as their carbohydrate-rich food reserve. Bees store pollen and honey in cells within the frames of the hive bodies.

Management: Beekeepers regularly inspect the hive bodies to assess the health and progress of the colony. They may conduct tasks such as monitoring brood development, managing population growth, and checking for signs of disease or pest infestation.

Expansion: Depending on the strength and needs of the colony, beekeepers may add additional hive bodies as the bees require more space for brood rearing or storage. The number of hive bodies used can vary depending on factors such as climate, available forage, and beekeeping objectives.

Hive bodies are a foundational component of a beehive, providing the essential living space for the honey bees. They support brood rearing, pollen and honey storage, and the overall growth and development of the colony.

Frames and foundation

Frames and foundation are important components of beehives that provide structure, support, and a guide for honey bees to build their comb.

Frames: Frames are wooden or plastic structures that hang vertically inside the hive bodies or supers of a beehive. They provide support for the beeswax comb that the honeybees construct to store honey, raise brood, and store pollen. Frames are designed to be removable, allowing beekeepers to inspect and manage the hive more easily.

Construction: Frames consist of a wooden or plastic frame with a top bar, bottom bar, and side bars. The size and dimensions of frames can vary depending on the hive design and beekeeping preferences. The frames are typically spaced evenly within the hive body, allowing the bees to build comb between them.

Foundation: Foundation is a thin sheet made of beeswax or plastic that is attached to the frames. It serves as a guide for the honeybees to build their comb in a predetermined pattern. Foundation provides a starting point for the bees, helping them save time and energy by following the template.

Wax Foundation: Beeswax foundation is traditionally used in beekeeping. It is made from thin sheets of beeswax imprinted with hexagonal cell patterns. These patterns mimic the natural comb structure created by bees in the wild. Wax foundation provides a familiar template for bees to build their comb and helps maintain uniform cell size.

Plastic Foundation: In recent years, plastic foundation has gained popularity due to its durability and ease of use. Plastic foundation is made of durable plastic sheets with preformed cell patterns. It offers consistent cell size and is resistant to pests and diseases. Plastic foundation is often used in combination with wooden frames.

Comb Building: Bees use the frames and foundation as a guide to construct their comb. They attach the foundation to the frame and then build the comb by drawing out wax cells from the foundation. The comb cells serve as storage areas for honey, pollen, and brood.

Management: Frames with foundation make hive management easier for beekeepers. They can be easily removed for inspection, honey extraction, or colony management tasks. The use of frames also helps prevent cross-combing, where bees build their comb in unintended locations, making hive manipulation more challenging.

Foundationless Frames: Some beekeepers opt for foundationless frames, where the frames are empty without any preformed foundation. With foundationless frames, bees build comb from scratch, allowing for natural cell size and pattern. However, this method requires more careful management to prevent cross-combing.

Frames and foundation provide structure and guidance for the honeybees to build their comb in a controlled manner. They facilitate the management of beehives, honey extraction, and brood inspection, enabling beekeepers to effectively care for their colonies and harvest honey while preserving the bees' natural instincts for comb construction.

Inner and outer covers

Inner and outer covers are components of a beehive that provide insulation, protection, and ventilation. Inner Cover: The inner cover is placed on top of the hive bodies or supers, just below the outer cover.

Ventilation: The inner cover typically has a small hole or notch that serves as an additional entrance and exit for the bees. This opening allows for proper ventilation within the hive, regulating temperature and humidity levels.

Insulation: The inner cover helps insulate the hive, providing an extra layer of protection against extreme temperatures. It helps maintain a more stable and optimal environment for the colony.

Feeding Access: In some beekeeping setups, the inner cover may have provisions for feeding the bees. This can include holes or slots for feeding jars or containers that provide supplemental food like sugar syrup or pollen patties.

Outer Cover: The outer cover, also known as a telescoping cover, is the topmost component of the beehive.

Protection from the Elements: The outer cover shields the hive from the weather, including rain, snow, and excessive sunlight. It helps prevent water from seeping into the hive and protects it from direct exposure to harsh environmental conditions.

Predator Defense: The outer cover helps deter predators, such as birds or mammals, from gaining easy access to the hive. It adds an additional layer of protection, making it more challenging for larger animals to disturb the colony.

Hive Security: The outer cover helps secure the hive, keeping the components in place and reducing the chances of unauthorized access or disturbance.

Overhang: The outer cover typically extends slightly beyond the edges of the hive bodies or supers. This overhang provides additional protection against rainwater runoff, ensuring that water does not enter the hive.

Both the inner and outer covers contribute to the overall health and well-being of the colony by maintaining a stable and protected hive environment. They work together with other hive components to regulate temperature, humidity, and ventilation, while safeguarding the bees and their resources from the elements and potential threats.

Protective clothing and gear

Bee suit or jacket

A bee suit or jacket is protective clothing worn by beekeepers to shield themselves from bee stings and minimize the risk of injury during hive inspections and other beekeeping activities.

Purpose: The primary purpose of a bee suit or jacket is to provide beekeepers with protection against bee stings. Honey bees can sting in defense when they perceive a threat to their colony, and beekeepers working with bees are at risk of being stung. Bee suits/jackets act as a barrier between the beekeeper's body and the bees, reducing the likelihood of stings and their associated discomfort and potential allergic reactions.

Design and Material: Bee suits/jackets are typically made from lightweight, breathable, and durable materials that offer protection while allowing ventilation. They are commonly constructed from a combination of cotton, polyester, or a synthetic blend. The material should be tightly woven to prevent bees from penetrating the fabric and stinging the beekeeper.

Components: Bee suits/jackets generally consist of the following components:

Jacket: The jacket is the upper part of the beekeeping protective clothing and covers the torso and arms. It usually has a zippered or Velcro closure at the front and may have elastic or adjustable cuffs at the wrists to prevent bees from entering the sleeves.

Veil: The veil is an integral part of the bee suit/jacket, protecting the beekeeper's face and neck from bee stings. It is typically made of a fine mesh material that allows for clear vision and adequate airflow while preventing bees from reaching the beekeeper's face. The veil can be attached to the jacket or worn separately as a standalone veil.

Hat or Hood: Some bee suits/jackets have an integrated hat or hood that provides additional protection for the beekeeper's head. The hat or hood usually has a mesh panel or fabric extension that covers the neck and offers full coverage around the head, ensuring that no exposed skin is accessible to bees.

Sizing and Fit: Bee suits/jackets are available in various sizes to accommodate different body shapes and heights. It is important to choose a suit/jacket that fits well to ensure maximum protection and comfort. The suit/jacket should be loose enough to allow freedom of movement but not so loose that bees can enter through gaps in the clothing.

Additional Features: Some bee suits/jackets may include additional features like reinforced knees, elastic ankle cuffs, or pockets for carrying beekeeping tools or personal items.

Maintenance and Care: Bee suits/jackets should be properly maintained and cleaned according to the manufacturer's instructions. Regular inspection for tears or holes in the fabric is important to ensure the integrity of the protective clothing. Keeping the suit/jacket clean and in good condition helps maintain its effectiveness and prolong its lifespan.

Bee suits/jackets are an essential component of a beekeeper's protective gear, offering a vital layer of defense against bee stings. By wearing a bee suit or jacket, beekeepers can work confidently and safely with their bees, minimizing the risk of stings and focusing on the care and management of their colonies.

Veil and gloves

In addition to the bee suit or jacket, beekeepers often wear a veil and gloves as essential protective gear when working with bees. Let's take a closer look at the veil and gloves used in beekeeping:

Veil: The veil is a protective covering that shields the beekeeper's face and neck from bee stings. It is typically made of a fine mesh material that allows for clear vision and adequate airflow while preventing bees from reaching the beekeeper's face. Here are some key points about veils:

Design: Veils come in different styles and designs. The most common type is a round veil that fits around the head and is secured to the jacket or worn separately. Another design is a fencing-style veil that extends further down, providing additional protection for the neck and shoulders.

Attachment: Veils are typically attached to the bee suit or jacket using zippers, Velcro, or drawstrings. They should be securely fastened to prevent bees from entering through gaps.

Structure: The veil is structured in a way that keeps the mesh material away from the face to avoid contact and potential bee stings. This is often achieved through the use of a wire or plastic frame that holds the mesh away from the beekeeper's skin.

Accessibility: Many veils have a zippered opening or flap that allows the beekeeper to access their face without fully removing the veil. This provides convenience for eating, drinking, or adjusting protective eyewear.

Gloves: Beekeeping gloves are worn to protect the beekeeper's hands and wrists from bee stings. They act as a barrier between the beekeeper and the bees, reducing the risk of stings and potential allergic reactions. Here are some important points about beekeeping gloves:

Material: Beekeeping gloves are typically made from leather or a synthetic material such as nitrile or latex. Leather gloves are durable and provide better protection against stings, while synthetic gloves offer more flexibility and are easier to clean.

Length: Beekeeping gloves are available in different lengths, ranging from wrist-length to elbow-length. The length of the gloves depends on personal preference and the desired level of protection. Longer gloves provide more coverage and protect a larger area of the arm.

Fit: It's important to choose gloves that fit properly. They should be snug enough to prevent bees from entering but not too tight to restrict movement or circulation. Proper fit ensures comfort and dexterity while working with the bees.

Sensitivity: Some beekeepers prefer thinner gloves or gloves with tactile sensitivity, as they allow for better control and manipulation of the hive components. Thinner gloves may provide less sting protection but can still offer sufficient coverage for many beekeeping tasks.

Handling: It's important to handle beekeeping gloves carefully to avoid inadvertently squishing bees or damaging comb during hive inspections. Some beekeepers may choose to remove gloves for delicate tasks that require more dexterity.

Both the veil and gloves are crucial components of a beekeeper's protective gear. They provide additional protection against bee stings to the face, neck, hands, and wrists. When used in combination with a bee suit or jacket, they help ensure the safety and comfort of the beekeeper while working with bees.

Smoker and hive tool

A smoker and hive tool are essential tools used by beekeepers during hive inspections and various beekeeping tasks. Let's explore their functions and how they are used:

Smoker: A smoker is a device that generates smoke, which is used to calm honeybees during hive inspections.

Purpose: The primary purpose of a smoker is to calm honeybees by disrupting their communication and defensive behavior. The smoke triggers a response in the bees, causing them to consume honey and become less aggressive.

Construction: Smokers are typically made of stainless steel or other heat-resistant materials. They consist of a firebox, bellows, and a nozzle. The firebox holds fuel, such as wood chips, pine needles, or cardboard, which is lit to produce smoke. The bellows are used to pump air into the firebox, forcing the smoke out through the nozzle.

How to Use: To use a smoker, the beekeeper first lights the fuel in the firebox until it produces a steady stream of smoke. The bellows are then pumped to maintain a consistent flow of smoke. The beekeeper directs the smoke into the hive entrance and around the frames to calm the bees. The smoke disrupts the bees' pheromone communication, making them less defensive.

Caution: It's important to use a smoker responsibly and with caution. Excessive smoke can stress the bees or even harm them. The goal is to use just enough smoke to calm the bees without causing unnecessary discomfort.

Hive Tool: A hive tool is a versatile tool used for various tasks in beekeeping. It is a handheld tool with a flat, thin, and slightly curved blade. Here's what you need to know about hive tools:

Functions: Hive tools serve multiple functions and are used for tasks such as:

Prying: The curved blade of the hive tool is used to pry apart hive components, such as separating supers or frames that may be stuck together due to propolis or wax buildup.

Scraping: The flat edge of the hive tool is used to scrape off excess propolis or wax from hive components. It helps remove unwanted debris or build-up, making it easier to inspect the hive.

Frame Manipulation: The notch or hook at the end of the hive tool is useful for lifting or manipulating frames within the hive. It allows beekeepers to remove frames for inspection, honey extraction, or colony management tasks.

Construction: Hive tools are typically made of stainless steel or other durable materials that can withstand the rigors of beekeeping. Some hive tools may have additional features, such as a nail-pulling notch or a small brush on the handle for cleaning purposes.

Handling: When using a hive tool, it's important to exercise caution and use it with precision to avoid damaging comb or injuring bees. Proper technique and control ensure efficient and safe manipulation of hive components.

Both the smoker and hive tool are indispensable tools for beekeepers. The smoker helps calm the bees during hive inspections, while the hive tool assists in opening hives, separating frames, and performing other necessary tasks. When used skillfully and responsibly, these tools contribute to the smooth and effective management of bee colonies.

Additional tools and supplies

A smoker and hive tool are essential tools used by beekeepers during hive inspections and various beekeeping tasks. Smoker: A smoker is a device that generates smoke, which is used to calm honeybees during hive inspections.

Purpose: The primary purpose of a smoker is to calm honeybees by disrupting their communication and defensive behavior. The smoke triggers a response in the bees, causing them to consume honey and become less aggressive.

Construction: Smokers are typically made of stainless steel or other heat-resistant materials. They consist of a firebox, bellows, and a nozzle. The firebox holds fuel, such as wood chips, pine needles, or cardboard, which is lit to produce smoke. The bellows are used to pump air into the firebox, forcing the smoke out through the nozzle.

How to Use: To use a smoker, the beekeeper first lights the fuel in the firebox until it produces a steady stream of smoke. The bellows are then pumped to maintain a consistent flow of smoke. The beekeeper directs the smoke into the hive entrance and around the frames to calm the bees. The smoke disrupts the bees' pheromone communication, making them less defensive.

Caution: It's important to use a smoker responsibly and with caution. Excessive smoke can stress the bees or even harm them. The goal is to use just enough smoke to calm the bees without causing unnecessary discomfort.

Hive Tool: A hive tool is a versatile tool used for various tasks in beekeeping. It is a handheld tool with a flat, thin, and slightly curved blade. Here's what you need to know about hive tools:

Functions: Hive tools serve multiple functions and are used for tasks such as:

Prying: The curved blade of the hive tool is used to pry apart hive components, such as separating supers or frames that may be stuck together due to propolis or wax buildup.

Scraping: The flat edge of the hive tool is used to scrape off excess propolis or wax from hive components. It helps remove unwanted debris or build-up, making it easier to inspect the hive.

Frame Manipulation: The notch or hook at the end of the hive tool is useful for lifting or manipulating frames within the hive. It allows beekeepers to remove frames for inspection, honey extraction, or colony management tasks.

Construction: Hive tools are typically made of stainless steel or other durable materials that can withstand the rigors of beekeeping. Some hive tools may have additional features, such as a nail-pulling notch or a small brush on the handle for cleaning purposes.

Handling: When using a hive tool, it's important to exercise caution and use it with precision to avoid damaging comb or injuring bees. Proper technique and control ensure efficient and safe manipulation of hive components.

Both the smoker and hive tool are indispensable tools for beekeepers. The smoker helps calm the bees during hive inspections, while the hive tool assists in opening hives, separating frames, and performing other necessary tasks. When used skillfully and responsibly, these tools contribute to the smooth and effective management of bee colonies.

Bee brush

A bee brush is a specialized tool used by beekeepers to gently brush bees off frames, hive components, or the beekeeper's clothing. It is designed to help manage the movement of bees during hive inspections without causing harm to them.

Purpose: The primary purpose of a bee brush is to remove bees from areas where they are not wanted, such as frames being inspected or removed from the hive. It allows the beekeeper to work with the frames more easily and minimizes the risk of accidentally squashing or injuring bees.

Design: A bee brush typically consists of soft bristles attached to a wooden or plastic handle. The bristles are usually made of natural fibers or synthetic materials. The brush head may have a gentle taper or be slightly curved to facilitate smooth brushing.

How to Use: When using a bee brush, the beekeeper gently brushes the bees off the surface or frame they want to work with. The soft bristles of the brush help dislodge the bees without causing harm. The bees will typically crawl away from the brush and onto other surfaces, allowing the beekeeper to proceed with their tasks.

Technique: It's important to use the bee brush with care and a light touch. The goal is to encourage the bees to move without applying excessive force that might harm them. Brushing too vigorously or crushing bees can cause stress and defensive behavior.

Handling: When using the bee brush, it's recommended to avoid direct contact with the bee's body. Gently sweeping or brushing the bees from the targeted area is sufficient. The brush should be used in a controlled manner to avoid flicking bees or damaging delicate structures like wings or legs.

Bee Brush Alternatives: While bee brushes are commonly used, some beekeepers prefer alternative methods to remove bees, such as blowing them gently with a puffer or using a bee blower. These methods can also be effective in moving bees away without causing harm.

Bee brushes are valuable tools for beekeepers, allowing them to manage bee movement and maintain a controlled environment during hive inspections. With proper use and technique, bee brushes help minimize bee stress and facilitate smoother beekeeping operations.

Honey extractor

A honey extractor is a mechanical device used by beekeepers to extract honey from honeycomb frames without damaging the comb. It works by utilizing centrifugal force to separate the honey from the cells.

Purpose: The primary purpose of a honey extractor is to efficiently extract honey from honeycomb frames while preserving the integrity of the comb. By using centrifugal force, the extractor removes the honey without damaging the cells, allowing the bees to reuse them.

Types: Honey extractors come in several types and sizes, including manual and electric models. Manual extractors require hand-cranking to spin the frames, while electric extractors are powered by electricity or battery, automating the spinning process.

Construction: Honey extractors are typically made of stainless steel, which is durable, hygienic, and easy to clean. The extractor consists of a drum or basket that holds the frames, a central spindle, and a handle or motor for rotation.

How it Works: To use a honey extractor, the beekeeper first removes the frames from the beehive. Uncapped frames are placed inside the extractor, either radially or tangentially. When the extractor is activated, it spins rapidly, causing the honey to be forced out of the comb due to centrifugal force. The extracted honey collects at the bottom of the extractor and can be collected through a tap or drain.

Extraction Process: Beekeepers often extract honey in stages. After spinning the frames on one side, they are flipped to extract the honey from the other side. This method ensures thorough extraction while minimizing damage to the comb.

Filtering: Once the honey is extracted, it may need to be filtered to remove any wax, propolis, or other impurities. Beekeepers typically use fine mesh filters or cheesecloth to achieve this.

Honeycomb Preservation: Honey extractors allow beekeepers to preserve the comb, which bees can reuse for storing honey or raising brood. By avoiding the need to crush and strain the comb, the bees can save time and energy that would otherwise be required to rebuild it.

It's important to note that honey extractors are an investment and are typically used by beekeepers who have established colonies producing sufficient honey for extraction. They enable beekeepers to efficiently harvest honey while maintaining the health of the hive and the quality of the comb.

Feeder and water source

Feeding bees and providing a water source are important aspects of beekeeping to ensure the well-being of the colony. Feeder: Bee feeders are used to provide supplemental food to honeybees when natural nectar sources are limited or unavailable. Feeders are especially useful during periods of low nectar flow, such as winter or drought.

Hive-Top Feeder: This feeder is placed on top of the hive, just beneath the outer cover. It consists of a container that holds the feed, such as sugar syrup or bee feed solution, and has access points for the bees to reach the feed. Hive-top feeders often have floats or ladder-like structures to prevent bees from drowning in the liquid feed.

Frame Feeder: Frame feeders are installed within the hive, replacing one or more frames in the brood chamber. They are shallow containers that hold the feed, allowing bees easy access from within the hive. Frame feeders typically have a lid or cap to prevent drowning.

Entrance Feeder: An entrance feeder is placed at the entrance of the hive. It is a small container or jar that holds the feed and has small holes or slits for the bees to access the liquid. Entrance feeders are easy to install and refill but may be more susceptible to robbing by other bees or pests.

Water Source: Providing a water source for bees is essential for their hydration and maintaining the optimal conditions within the hive.

Some considerations for establishing a water source:

Proximity: The water source should be located relatively close to the beehives to minimize the bees' flight distance and reduce the risk of them seeking water from neighboring properties or potentially unsafe areas.

Accessibility: Bees require a water source that is shallow and provides a landing surface. Having a landing platform, such as a floating platform with rocks or twigs, allows the bees to access the water easily without drowning.

Cleanliness: The water source should be clean and free from chemicals or contaminants that may harm the bees. Avoid using water sources treated with pesticides or chemicals. Providing fresh water or regularly changing and cleaning the water helps maintain a healthy environment for the bees.

Alternatives: Some beekeepers use dedicated bee watering stations, such as small bird baths or shallow dishes filled with water and rocks for the bees to land on. Others provide water sources in the form of damp soil or by allowing rainwater to collect in certain areas.

Both feeders and water sources play important roles in supporting the health and vitality of bee colonies. Beekeepers should monitor and replenish feeders regularly and ensure that water sources are available throughout the year, particularly during times when natural resources are limited.

Chapter 4. Selecting Honey Bee Species

Common honey bee species

There are several common honey bee species, each with its own characteristics and traits.

Apis mellifera: This species is the most widespread and commonly kept honey bee species worldwide. It includes various subspecies or breeds that have adapted to different regions and climates. Some popular subspecies of Apis mellifera include:

Italian honey bees (Apis mellifera ligustica): Known for their gentle temperament, large brood population, and high honey production. They are popular among beekeepers for their productivity and ease of management.

Carniolan honey bees (Apis mellifera carnica): Originating from Central Europe, Carniolan bees are known for their calm behavior, adaptability to colder climates, and resistance to Varroa mites. They are favored by beekeepers in regions with cooler climates and shorter summers.

Caucasian honey bees (Apis mellifera caucasica): Native to the Caucasus region, Caucasian bees are known for their gentle temperament, strong brood production, and ability to withstand colder climates. They are valued for their honey production and overwintering capabilities.

Apis cerana: This species, commonly known as the Eastern honeybee or the Asian honeybee, is native to Asia, including parts of India, Southeast Asia, and China. Apis cerana is smaller in size compared to Apis mellifera and has different behavioral characteristics. It has adapted to a range of environments and has been used for honey production and pollination in its native range.

Apis dorsata: Also known as the Giant honeybee, Apis dorsata is one of the largest honeybee species. It is native to South and Southeast Asia and is known for building large single-comb nests in open locations, such as tree branches. Apis dorsata is primarily wild and less commonly kept by beekeepers.

Apis florea: Commonly known as the Dwarf honeybee, Apis florea is the smallest honey bee species. It is native to Southeast Asia and is known for its small colony size and nesting behavior in small cavities, such as tree branches and crevices.

It's important to note that the suitability of honeybee species may vary depending on the specific geographical location, climate, and beekeeping objectives. Local beekeeping associations or experienced beekeepers in your area can provide valuable insights and recommendations regarding the most appropriate honeybee species for your specific region and circumstances.

Factors to consider when choosing a species

Climate: Consider the climate of your region, including temperature, humidity, and seasonal variations. Some honeybee species are more suited to specific climates than others. For example, certain breeds are better adapted to colder or hotter climates, while others are more resilient to humidity or drought.

Availability and Local Adaptation: Consider the availability of honeybee species in your area. It's generally recommended to choose species or subspecies that are already established in your region. Local honeybees may have developed adaptations to local environmental conditions and have a better chance of thriving.

Productivity: Evaluate the honey production capabilities of different honeybee species. Some species are known for their high honey yields, while others may prioritize other traits like pollination or propolis production. Consider your beekeeping goals and the desired honey production level when selecting a species.

Temperament: Honeybee temperament can vary among species and subspecies. Some bees are known for their gentle and calm behavior, while others may be more defensive or prone to swarming. Consider the temperament of the bees and how it aligns with your comfort level and beekeeping practices.

Disease Resistance: Be aware of the disease resistance traits of different honey bee species. Some species or subspecies may exhibit natural resistance to specific pests and diseases, such as Varroa mites or American foulbrood. Choosing bees with inherent resistance or tolerance can help reduce the need for chemical treatments and promote healthier colonies.

Management Requirements: Different honeybee species may have varying management requirements. Consider the time, effort, and resources you are willing to invest in beekeeping. Some species may require more intensive management, while others are more self-sufficient or less demanding.

Local Regulations: Check if there are any local regulations or restrictions on the importation or keeping of specific honeybee species. Some regions have regulations in place to prevent the introduction of non-native species or to protect local bee populations.

It's important to consult with local beekeeping associations, experienced beekeepers, or agricultural extension offices in your area for guidance on selecting the most suitable honey bee species. They can provide valuable insights based on their knowledge of local conditions and beekeeping practices.

Climate suitability

When selecting a honeybee species for beekeeping, climate suitability is an important factor to consider. Honeybees are adapted to different climates and have varying abilities to thrive in specific environmental conditions.

Apis mellifera: The Apis mellifera species, which includes various subspecies or breeds, is the most widely kept honey bee species worldwide. Different subspecies have developed adaptations to various climates. Here are some examples:

Italian honey bees (Apis mellifera ligustica): They are well-suited for temperate climates with moderate temperatures and abundant forage. Italian honey bees thrive in regions with mild winters and long, warm summers.

Carniolan honey bees (Apis mellifera carnica): These bees are highly adaptable and perform well in colder climates. They have a reputation for overwintering successfully and tolerating cooler temperatures compared to other subspecies.

Buckfast bees: Developed by Brother Adam, Buckfast bees are hybrids that incorporate genetic traits from various honey bee subspecies. They have been bred to adapt to different climates and are known for their resilience and productivity.

Apis cerana: Apis cerana, also known as the Eastern honeybee or the Asian honeybee, is native to Asia. It is well-adapted to tropical and subtropical climates, including regions with high humidity and temperatures. Apis cerana is not as commonly kept as Apis mellifera but is suitable for beekeeping in its native range.

Local Adaptations: In addition to specific honeybee species, local adaptations within a species may exist. Bees that have been bred and selected within a specific region over time may exhibit better tolerance to local climate conditions, pests, and diseases. Local beekeeping associations and experienced beekeepers can provide insights into the honeybee strains or subspecies that have adapted well to your specific area.

It's important to consider the climate conditions of your region, including factors such as temperature ranges, humidity levels, precipitation patterns, and forage availability. Matching the honeybee species or subspecies to the local climate can increase the chances of success in beekeeping. Consulting with local beekeeping associations, experienced beekeepers, or agricultural extension offices in your area can provide valuable guidance on which honeybee species are best suited to your specific climate conditions.

Temperament and behavior

The temperament and behavior of honeybees can vary among different species and subspecies. It's important to consider these factors when selecting honey bees for beekeeping.

Gentleness: Some honeybee species or subspecies are known for their gentle temperament, meaning they are less likely to exhibit aggressive or defensive behavior. This can make them more manageable and less prone to stinging. Italian honey bees (Apis mellifera ligustica) and Carniolan honey bees (Apis mellifera carnica) are often considered gentle breeds.

Defensiveness: Other honeybee species or subspecies may be more defensive and prone to stinging, especially when they perceive a threat to the hive. Africanized honeybees (AHBs), often referred to as "killer bees," are known for their highly defensive nature. However, it's important to note that the majority of honeybee colonies, regardless of species, are not overly aggressive if properly managed.

Swarming: Swarming is a natural reproductive process of honeybees. Some honeybee breeds are more prone to swarming than others. Swarming is a colony's way of reproducing by splitting into two or more colonies. While swarming behavior is a natural process, beekeepers may prefer breeds that have a lower tendency to swarm to prevent potential disruptions and loss of bees.

Work Ethic and Productivity: Honeybees are industrious and diligent workers. Some breeds are known for their strong work ethic and high productivity in terms of honey production, brood rearing, and foraging capabilities. The productivity of honeybee colonies can vary based on genetics, environmental conditions, and management practices.

Hygienic Behavior: Some honeybee breeds exhibit hygienic behavior, which refers to their ability to detect and remove diseased or dead broods from the hive. This behavior can contribute to the overall health and hygiene of the colony and may help in managing diseases and pests.

It's important to note that the temperament and behavior of honeybees can be influenced by factors such as genetics, environmental conditions, queen quality, and management practices. Additionally, individual colonies within a specific honeybee breed can also exhibit variations in temperament and behavior.

When selecting honeybees, consider your personal preferences, level of experience, and beekeeping objectives. Consult with local beekeeping associations, experienced beekeepers, or breeders to gather insights on the temperament and behavior of different honey bee breeds in your region. They can provide valuable guidance and recommendations based on their knowledge and experience with specific honeybee breeds.

Disease resistance

Disease resistance is an important consideration when choosing honey bee species or subspecies for beekeeping. Honeybees can be susceptible to various pests and diseases that can impact the health and productivity of the colony.

Varroa Mites: Varroa destructor is one of the most significant pests affecting honey bees worldwide. These parasitic mites can weaken honeybee colonies, transmit viruses, and lead to colony losses if left untreated. Some honeybee breeds have developed certain traits that make them more resistant or tolerant to varroa mite infestations. Breeds like the Russian honey bees (Apis mellifera carnica) and the VSH (Varroa Sensitive Hygiene) strains have been selected for their ability to groom, detect, and remove mites from the hive.

Other Pests: Honeybees can be affected by other pests such as the small hive beetle, wax moths, and tracheal mites. While some honeybee breeds may exhibit certain levels of resistance or behaviors that help manage these pests, it's important to employ proper hive management techniques and integrated pest management strategies to control and prevent infestations.

Disease Tolerance: Honeybees can also be susceptible to various diseases, including bacterial infections (e.g., American foulbrood), fungal infections (e.g., chalkbrood), and viral infections (e.g., deformed wing virus). While no honeybee breed is completely immune to all diseases, certain strains or subspecies may exhibit better tolerance or resistance to specific diseases.

Local Adaptation: Honeybees that have been bred and selected within a specific region over time may have developed some degree of resistance or tolerance to local pests and diseases. Locally adapted bees may have traits that make them better suited to the prevailing environmental conditions and challenges in your area.

It's important to note that disease resistance is not the sole factor to consider when selecting honey bees for beekeeping. Other factors such as temperament, productivity, and climate suitability should also be taken into account. Consulting with local beekeeping associations, experienced beekeepers, or breeders in your area can provide insights into the disease resistance traits of different honeybee strains and subspecies that are well-suited to your specific region and management practices. Additionally, implementing good hive management practices, monitoring for diseases, and practicing biosecurity measures can help maintain healthy colonies regardless of the honeybee breed chosen.

Chapter 5. Choosing a Suitable Location

Choosing a suitable location for your beehives is crucial for the success of your beekeeping endeavor.

Forage Availability: Bees require access to a diverse and abundant source of nectar and pollen. Look for locations with a variety of flowering plants, trees, and crops that can provide a consistent and ample food supply throughout the year. Consider the availability of natural forage as well as the proximity to agricultural areas or gardens.

Water Source: Bees need a nearby water source for drinking and cooling the hive. Ensure there is a clean and reliable water source, such as a pond, stream, or birdbath, within a reasonable distance from the beehives. Provide a water source with a shallow landing area or place floating objects, such as rocks or twigs, to prevent bees from drowning.

Sun Exposure: Bees thrive in sunny locations that receive adequate sunlight throughout the day. Select a site that gets at least six hours of direct sunlight daily. Sunlight helps bees regulate the temperature inside the hive and promotes healthy brood development.

Wind Protection: Strong winds can disrupt bees' flight and make foraging more challenging. Choose a location that offers some natural windbreaks, such as trees, hedges, or buildings, to provide protection from strong winds. However, ensure there is still sufficient airflow to prevent excessive heat buildup in the hive during hot weather.

Accessibility: Consider the accessibility of the beehives for regular inspections, maintenance, and honey harvesting. Ensure there is enough space around the hives for you to work comfortably and safely. Keep in mind that beekeeping equipment and tools require storage space as well.

Land Ownership and Permission: Ensure that you have legal permission to keep bees on the chosen property. If you own the land, this should not be an issue. However, if you are planning to place hives on someone else's property, obtain written permission from the landowner and discuss any concerns they may have.

Regulations and Zoning: Check local ordinances and zoning regulations regarding beekeeping. Some areas have specific rules and restrictions on the number of hives allowed, setback requirements, and proximity to residential areas. Ensure that your chosen location complies with local regulations to avoid potential conflicts.

Neighbors and Public Safety: Consider the proximity of neighboring properties and potential public safety concerns. Be mindful of any allergies to bee stings and ensure that the beehives are not located too close to areas with heavy foot traffic or where people may gather.

Environmental Considerations: Take into account the surrounding environment and any potential risks to the bees, such as exposure to pesticides, chemical runoff, or other pollutants. Avoid placing hives in areas with high levels of agricultural chemical usage or industrial pollution.

By considering these factors, you can select a suitable location that provides the necessary resources and conditions for your bees to thrive while minimizing potential conflicts with neighbors and adhering to local regulations. Consulting with local beekeeping associations, experienced beekeepers, or agricultural extension offices can provide valuable guidance specific to your region.

Considerations for hive placement

When placing your beehives, there are several considerations to keep in mind to ensure the well-being of your bees and the success of your beekeeping operation.

Stability and Level Ground: Choose a location with stable and level ground to provide a solid foundation for your beehives. This will help prevent the hives from tipping over, ensuring the safety of the bees and the structural integrity of the hives.

Adequate Air Circulation: Bees require good airflow to regulate the temperature and humidity inside the hive. Avoid placing hives in areas with stagnant air or poor ventilation. Adequate air circulation helps prevent excessive heat buildup in the summer and condensation issues in colder months.

Orientation: Face the hive entrance towards the southeast if possible. This allows the bees to take advantage of the morning sun, which helps to warm up the hive and stimulate foraging activity. However, the specific orientation may depend on the local climate and prevailing winds.

Distance from High-Traffic Areas: Place your beehives away from high-traffic areas, such as walkways, playgrounds, and gathering spots. This helps minimize the risk of bee-human interactions and potential stinging incidents. Consider the flight path of the bees and ensure they have a clear and unobstructed pathway.

Vegetation and Forage: Surrounding vegetation plays a crucial role in providing forage for your bees. Look for areas with a diverse range of flowering plants and trees that can offer a consistent and abundant food source throughout the seasons. Avoid locations with limited floral resources or areas where pesticides are heavily used.

Protection from Extreme Weather: Provide some natural or man-made protection from extreme weather conditions. This can include windbreaks, such as trees or fences, to shield the hives from strong winds, or shade structures to protect the hives from excessive heat and direct sunlight.

Accessibility for Management: Ensure the hives are easily accessible for regular hive inspections, maintenance, and honey harvesting. Leave enough space around the hives to work comfortably and safely and consider the storage of beekeeping equipment and tools.

Water Source: Place your beehives within a reasonable distance from a clean and reliable water source. Bees require water for hydration and cooling the hive. Having a water source nearby reduces the bees' need to venture far and minimizes the risk of them seeking water from less desirable locations, such as swimming pools or pet water bowls.

Consider Neighbors: Be considerate of your neighbors and their proximity to the beehives. Place the hives in a location that minimizes any potential disturbances or conflicts. Communicate with neighbors about your beekeeping activities and address any concerns they may have.

Remember to check and comply with any local regulations or guidelines regarding hive placement, setback requirements, or proximity to neighboring properties. Consulting with experienced beekeepers or local beekeeping associations can provide valuable insights and recommendations specific to your area.

Access to sunlight

Temperature Regulation: Bees need sunlight to regulate the temperature inside the hive. Sunlight warms up the hive, particularly in cooler climates, helping to maintain optimal temperatures for brood rearing and overall colony health. Adequate warmth is essential for the development of larvae and the proper functioning of the hive.

Hive Sterilization: Sunlight has natural sterilizing properties that can help in keeping the hive clean and reducing the spread of certain diseases and pests. Sunlight exposure can help dry out and sanitize the interior of the hive, reducing the chances of mold and bacterial growth.

Hive Orientation and Foraging: Placing the hive in a location that receives ample sunlight helps with hive orientation and foraging efficiency. Bees rely on the position of the sun as a navigational reference when leaving and returning to the hive. Having the hive in a sunny location makes it easier for the bees to orient themselves and find their way back.

Aim for a location that receives at least six hours of direct sunlight per day, especially during the morning hours. This allows the bees to warm up and become active earlier in the day, maximizing foraging opportunities.

Ensure that the beehives are not completely exposed to harsh, direct sunlight all day long, particularly in hot climates. Provide some shade or a partial shade structure to prevent excessive heat buildup inside the hive, which can stress the bees.

Take into account the sun's path throughout the year. Observe how the sun moves across the potential hive location during different seasons to ensure that it will receive adequate sunlight year-round.

Consider the surrounding landscape and structures that may cast shadows and impact the amount of sunlight reaching the hives. Avoid placing the hives in the shadow of tall trees, buildings, or other structures that can obstruct sunlight.

Balancing sunlight exposure and providing some shade when needed is essential for maintaining a suitable temperature and environment within the hive. Monitoring the hive's temperature and observing the behavior of the bees can help determine if adjustments need to be made to optimize sunlight exposure.

Remember to also consider other factors like forage availability, wind protection, and accessibility when choosing the final hive placement. Consulting with experienced beekeepers or local beekeeping associations can provide additional guidance specific to your region and climate.

Protection from strong winds

Protection from strong winds is an important consideration when placing beehives.

Hive Stability: Strong winds can topple or destabilize beehives, leading to potential damage to the hive structure and the bees themselves. Ensuring hive stability is crucial for the safety and well-being of the bees.

Preventing Cold Drafts: Strong winds can create drafts that can enter the hive, causing temperature fluctuations and making it difficult for bees to maintain a consistent and optimal hive temperature. Cold drafts can stress the bees and impact their ability to survive winter or inclement weather.

Minimizing Foraging Challenges: Bees face challenges when flying in strong winds, such as increased energy expenditure and difficulty in navigating back to the hive. Providing wind protection can help reduce these challenges and make foraging more efficient for the bees.

Natural Windbreaks: Utilize natural windbreaks, such as trees, hedges, or shrubs, to shield the beehives from strong winds. These natural barriers can help block or redirect the wind, providing a more sheltered location for the hives.

Fence or Wall: Consider placing the hives near a solid fence or wall that can act as a windbreak. This can help reduce the impact of strong winds and create a more protected microclimate around the hives.

Windbreak Fabric or Boards: Install windbreak fabric or boards on the windward side of the hives to create a physical barrier against the wind. This can help divert or reduce the force of the wind hitting the hives directly.

Strategic Placement: Observe the wind patterns in the area where you plan to place the hives. Position the hives in a location that is naturally sheltered or shielded from prevailing winds. This may involve selecting a site that is protected by existing structures or contours of the land.

Hive Orientation: Consider how you orient the hive entrance in relation to the prevailing wind direction. While it's generally recommended to face the hive entrance towards the southeast for morning sun exposure, you may want to slightly adjust the orientation to provide some protection against strong winds.

Hive Weight and Stability: Ensure that the hive components are securely fastened and weighted down to prevent them from toppling over in strong winds. Heavy hive bodies and secure hive stands or pallets can help improve stability.

Monitor Hive Conditions: Regularly inspect the hives to assess any wind-related issues or damage. Make necessary adjustments or repairs promptly to maintain hive integrity and protect the bees.

Keep in mind that some airflow is still necessary to prevent excessive moisture buildup inside the hive. Avoid completely enclosing the hives, as it can lead to ventilation issues and humidity problems. Finding the right balance between wind protection and proper ventilation is key.

Consider the specific wind patterns and intensity in your area, as wind conditions can vary greatly depending on the region and local topography. Consulting with experienced local beekeepers or beekeeping associations can provide valuable insights on wind protection strategies that are effective in your specific area.

By providing adequate wind protection, you can help ensure the stability and comfort of the beehives, creating a more favorable environment for your bees to thrive.

Distance from neighbors and public areas.

Bee Flight Path: Bees typically fly in a straight line when leaving and returning to the hive. It's important to ensure that the flight path of the bees doesn't intersect with heavily trafficked areas or areas where people frequently gather. Placing the hives a sufficient distance away from neighbors and public areas helps minimize the risk of bee-human interactions and potential stinging incidents.

Safety Considerations: Some individuals may have allergies or sensitivities to bee stings. Keeping the hives at a safe distance from neighbors and public areas helps reduce the chances of accidental stings and potential allergic reactions. It's considerate to keep a respectful distance to minimize any potential risks.

Privacy and Aesthetics: Placing the hives a reasonable distance away from neighboring properties and public areas can help maintain privacy for both you and your neighbors. This ensures that the beekeeping activity doesn't encroach on their space or cause discomfort. It also helps maintain a visually pleasing environment for everyone involved.

Local Regulations and Zoning: Check local ordinances and regulations regarding minimum distance requirements for beehives from neighboring properties and public areas. Some jurisdictions may have specific guidelines on hive placement to address potential concerns or conflicts. Adhering to these regulations helps maintain a harmonious relationship with neighbors and ensures compliance with local laws.

Open Communication: It's essential to communicate with your neighbors about your beekeeping activities. Inform them about your plans to keep bees, explain the benefits of bees for pollination and the environment, and address any concerns they may have. Open dialogue and transparency can help foster understanding and cooperation.

Remember that the optimal distance between hives and neighbors/public areas may vary depending on local conditions, such as the density of the population, land size, and local regulations. It's advisable to consult with experienced beekeepers or local beekeeping associations to get insights specific to your area.

By considering the distance from neighbors and public areas, you can create a beekeeping setup that promotes a harmonious relationship with the community while ensuring the safety and comfort of both your bees and the people around you.

Providing a water source

Providing a water source for your bees is crucial for their well-being and survival. Bees require water for various purposes, including cooling the hive, diluting honey, and hydration.

Accessibility: Ensure that the water source is easily accessible to the bees. Place it within a reasonable distance from the beehives, ideally within a 50-foot radius. Bees are more likely to use a water source that is closer to their hive, reducing the chances of them seeking water from less desirable locations, such as swimming pools or bird baths.

Fresh and Clean Water: Bees prefer fresh, clean water. Provide a shallow water source that allows bees to land and access the water easily without the risk of drowning. It's best to use a container or shallow basin with a textured surface or floating objects (e.g., rocks or twigs) that serve as landing platforms for the bees.

Water Depth: Bees can drown in deep water sources, so it's important to ensure the water is shallow. Aim for a depth of around 1 to 2 inches (2.5 to 5 centimeters). Placing small rocks or pebbles in the water source can provide additional landing surfaces and prevent bees from submerging.

Clean and Refresh: Regularly clean and refresh the water source to prevent the growth of algae or the accumulation of debris. Bees are attracted to clean water, and a dirty water source may discourage them from using it. Replace the water every few days, especially during hot weather, to maintain its freshness.

Avoid Chemical Contamination: Ensure that the water source is free from chemical contaminants, such as pesticides or herbicides. Bees are sensitive to chemicals, and contaminated water can harm their health. Choose a location for the water source away from areas where chemicals are used or consider using filtered or collected rainwater.

Multiple Water Sources: If possible, provide multiple water sources in your beekeeping area. This helps prevent overcrowding and reduces competition among the bees for access to water. Having multiple water sources also ensures a consistent supply, especially during periods of high bee activity.

Dripping or Misting System: Consider installing a dripping or misting system near the water source. Bees are attracted to moving water, and these systems can mimic the effect of rain or a natural water source, making it more enticing for the bees to visit and use the water source.

Bee-Friendly Landscaping: Create a bee-friendly environment around the water source by planting suitable flowering plants nearby. This helps attract bees to the area and provides additional forage opportunities. Avoid using pesticides or herbicides in the vicinity of the water source and surrounding vegetation.

Regularly monitor the water source to ensure that it is being utilized by the bees. You can observe bee activity around the water source and check for signs of dehydration or inadequate water supply within the hive.

Providing a reliable and accessible water source for your bees contributes to their overall health and productivity. It also helps prevent them from seeking water from potentially problematic locations, minimizing any conflicts with neighbors or other areas where people gather.

Ensuring forage availability

Ensuring forage availability is essential for the health and productivity of your bees. Bees rely on nectar and pollen from flowering plants as their primary sources of food.

Plant Diverse Floral Sources: Aim for a diverse range of flowering plants in your beekeeping area. Different plants bloom at different times of the year, providing a continuous and varied supply of nectar and pollen throughout the seasons. Choose plants that are known to attract bees and provide abundant nectar and pollen, such as lavender, sunflowers, clover, borage, and wildflowers.

Native Plants: Incorporate native plants into your landscape as they are well-adapted to the local climate and provide natural forage for local bee populations. Native plants often have a higher nectar and pollen content, making them valuable food sources for bees.

Seasonal Blooms: Ensure that there are flowering plants available for bees during each season. Plan your planting to provide a succession of blooms from spring to fall, allowing bees to find food throughout the year. This helps sustain the bee colony's nutritional needs and supports their population growth.

Pollinator-Friendly Practices: Avoid using pesticides, herbicides, and fungicides in your beekeeping area. These chemicals can be harmful to bees and other pollinators. Instead, opt for organic and bee-friendly pest management practices. Additionally, consider creating pesticide-free zones or encouraging your neighbors to adopt pollinator-friendly practices.

Beekeeping Co-op: Collaborate with local farmers, gardeners, or fellow beekeepers to establish a cooperative effort in providing forage for bees. By working together, you can create larger forage areas and diversify the available food sources. This also facilitates knowledge sharing and strengthens the local beekeeping community.

Water Availability: As mentioned earlier, ensure a nearby water source for your bees. Bees need water for hydration and regulating the temperature of their hives. A readily available water source close to the beehives reduces the risk of bees venturing farther in search of water, ensuring they stay focused on foraging within their immediate surroundings.

Seasonal Management: Be mindful of the specific forage needs of your bees during different seasons. Conduct regular inspections and monitor the availability of nectar and pollen. If necessary, supplement their diet with sugar syrup or pollen substitutes during periods of low natural forage availability.

Evaluate Local Conditions: Consider the local climate, soil conditions, and availability of natural resources when planning forage availability. Certain plants may thrive better in specific regions, and understanding the local ecosystem will help you select suitable plants for your beekeeping area.

By ensuring forage availability, you provide your bees with the necessary nutrition for their growth, honey production, and overall health. It also helps support the local ecosystem and contributes to the pollination of nearby plants and crops. Collaborating with local gardening and conservation groups can provide valuable insights and resources for creating a bee-friendly environment.

Chapter 6. Installing and Managing Bees

Installing and managing bees in your beehives is an exciting and crucial part of beekeeping.

Acquiring Bees: There are several ways to acquire bees for your hives. You can purchase packaged bees, which typically include a queen and a certain number of worker bees in a screened package. Alternatively, you can purchase nucleus colonies (nucs), which are small, established colonies with a queen, workers, brood, and resources. Another option is to catch a swarm or obtain bees from a local beekeeper. Choose a reputable source to ensure healthy and disease-free bees.

Hive Preparation: Before installing the bees, make sure your hive equipment is properly prepared. Clean the hive components and assemble them according to the manufacturer's instructions. Ensure that frames are inserted into the hive bodies and have a foundation or comb drawn by bees for the bees to start building on.

Installation Process:

a. Select a suitable time to install the bees, preferably during a mild and calm day when bees are active but not overly agitated. b. Place the hive in its final location before installing the bees. c. Remove the top cover and any inner covers from the hive. d. If using packaged bees, remove the queen cage and carefully release the queen into the hive. Alternatively, if using a nuc, carefully transfer the frames with bees, brood, and resources from the nuc to the hive. e. Inspect each frame to ensure the queen is safely released into the hive and the bees are settling in. f. Close the hive by replacing the frames, inner cover, and top cover.

Monitoring and Care: Once the bees are installed, regular monitoring and care are essential for their well-being. Here are some key aspects of bee management:

a. Inspections: Conduct regular hive inspections to monitor the health and development of the colony. Inspect for signs of disease, pests, and the queen's performance. Check for sufficient food stores, brood development, and population strength.

b. Feeding: If necessary, provide supplemental feeding to the bees during periods of low natural forage availability or when establishing a new colony. Sugar syrup can be provided as a substitute for nectar, and pollen substitutes can be offered to supplement pollen intake.

c. Pest and Disease Management: Implement appropriate pest and disease management practices to keep the colony healthy. This includes monitoring for varroa mites, inspecting for signs of diseases like American foulbrood or European foulbrood, and taking necessary actions to control or treat issues that arise.

d. Hive Maintenance: Regularly maintain and repair the hive equipment as needed. Ensure that frames are in good condition, replace any damaged components, and provide adequate ventilation in the hive.

e. Swarm Prevention: Monitor the hive for signs of swarming, such as the presence of queen cells. Take necessary steps to prevent swarming, such as providing additional space, managing the hive's population, or performing a split to create a new colony.

Record Keeping: Maintain detailed records of hive inspections, hive health, honey production, and other relevant observations. Keeping records helps track the progress of the colony, identify patterns or issues, and make informed management decisions.

Remember, bee management practices may vary depending on the specific needs of your bees, your location, and local conditions. It's important to continually educate yourself, stay updated on best practices, and seek guidance from experienced beekeepers or local beekeeping associations.

By installing and managing bees in your beehives with care and attention, you can create a healthy and thriving bee colony that will reward you with honey production, pollination

Acquiring bees

Acquiring bees is an important step in starting your beekeeping journey.

Purchasing Packaged Bees: Packaged bees are a popular option for beginner beekeepers. They typically come in a screened package containing a certain number of worker bees and a mated queen. Packaged bees are usually available for purchase from reputable bee suppliers or local beekeeping associations. The package can be installed into a prepared hive, and the bees will establish their colony.

Buying Nucleus Colonies (Nucs): Nucleus colonies, or nucs, are small established colonies consisting of a mated queen, several frames of brood, bees, and food stores. Nucs provide a head start compared to packaged bees, as they already have a laying queen, established worker population, and developing brood. You can purchase nucs from experienced beekeepers, local beekeeping associations, or bee suppliers.

Catching Swarms: Swarms occur when a colony divides, and a portion of bees, along with a queen, leave the original hive in search of a new home. Beekeepers often capture swarms to increase their bee colonies. You can catch swarms yourself or contact local beekeepers or beekeeping associations who may assist in capturing swarms. Swarming season varies depending on the region and climate.

Splitting Existing Colonies: If you have an established colony, you can create new colonies by splitting the existing one. This involves taking frames with brood, bees, and food stores and placing them in a separate hive with a new queen or queen cells. Splitting colonies is a method of expanding your beekeeping operation, but it requires knowledge and experience to ensure the success of both the original and new colonies.

Local Beekeeper Networking: Reach out to local beekeepers or beekeeping associations in your area. They may have surplus bees or know of other beekeepers looking to sell bees or nucs. Networking with experienced beekeepers provides an opportunity to learn from their expertise and potentially acquire bees from reliable sources.

When acquiring bees, it's essential to select healthy and disease-free colonies.

Choose reputable suppliers or individuals who prioritize the health and well-being of their bees. Consider local climate and beekeeping conditions when acquiring bees to ensure they are well-suited for your region.

Remember to check local regulations and any specific requirements or restrictions regarding the acquisition of bees in your area. By acquiring bees from reliable sources and establishing strong colonies, you'll set a solid foundation for a successful beekeeping endeavor.

Purchasing packages or nucs (nucleus colonies)

Purchasing packaged bees or nucleus colonies (nucs) are two common methods of acquiring bees for your beekeeping operation. Here's an overview of these options:

Packaged Bees:

Packaged bees typically come in a screened package containing a certain weight or number of worker bees and a mated queen.

They are usually sold in the spring season when bee populations are actively growing and beekeepers are looking to expand their colonies or establish new ones.

Packaged bees are commonly available from reputable bee suppliers, local beekeeping associations, or through online beekeeping retailers.

When purchasing packaged bees, ensure they come from a trusted source that prioritizes the health and quality of their bees. Look for suppliers who have good reviews and a track record of providing healthy packages.

Packaged bees are typically installed into a prepared hive by shaking or pouring the bees into the hive and placing the queen cage inside for the bees to release her gradually.

It's important to closely monitor the newly installed package to ensure the queen is accepted, the colony is establishing well, and there are no signs of disease or issues.

Nucleus Colonies (Nucs):

Nucs are small, established colonies that consist of several frames of brood (eggs, larvae, and capped cells), bees, food stores, and a mated queen.

They provide a head start compared to packaged bees since they already have a laying queen, worker population, and developing brood.

Nucs are typically sold in wooden or cardboard nucleus boxes and are ready to be transferred to a permanent hive.

Nucs are sought after by beekeepers because they offer a more established and self-sustaining colony from the start.

You can purchase nucs from local beekeepers, beekeeping associations, or reputable bee suppliers.

When buying nucs, inspect them for overall colony health, the presence of a laying queen, and sufficient bees and resources. Ensure that the nucs are free from diseases or pests.

Transferring a nuc to a permanent hive involves carefully moving the frames, along with the bees and queen, into the new hive and providing additional frames and space for expansion.

Nucs may be available for purchase at different times of the year depending on the local beekeeping season and availability of colonies.

When considering whether to purchase packaged bees or nucs, take into account your level of experience, the desired size of the colony you wish to start with, and your local beekeeping conditions. Both options have their advantages and can be successful when sourced from reliable suppliers or reputable beekeepers. It's important to ensure the health and quality of the bees you acquire to set a strong foundation for your beekeeping venture.

Capturing swarms or performing hive splits

Capturing swarms and performing hive splits are two methods of acquiring bees that involve utilizing existing bee colonies.

Capturing Swarms:

1. Swarming is a natural process in which a portion of bees, along with a queen, leave the original hive to establish a new colony.

2. Capturing swarms allows you to acquire bees without purchasing them, making it a cost-effective method.

3. Swarms are most commonly found during the spring and early summer when bee populations are strong and colonies are expanding.

4.

a. Set up swarm traps or bait hives in strategic locations to attract passing swarms. These traps are typically empty hives or boxes with frames and some lure, such as old comb or essential oils.

b.

5. Respond to swarm calls or notifications from local beekeeping associations or community members. Swarms may be clustered on trees, fences, or other structures, and you can carefully collect them and transfer them into a prepared hive.

6. When capturing a swarm, it's important to ensure you have the necessary equipment, including a bee suit, a bee brush, a hive tool, and a suitable hive to transfer the swarm into.

7. Once captured, the swarm can be transferred into a prepared hive, and additional frames and resources can be provided to support their establishment.

Performing Hive Splits:

1. Hive splitting involves dividing an existing colony into two or more separate colonies.

2. Hive splits are typically done by experienced beekeepers who have knowledge of colony management and bee behavior.

3. By performing a split, you can increase your number of colonies, prevent swarming, or create new colonies for various purposes.

4. Identify a strong and healthy colony with a sufficient population and resources.

5. Prepare a new hive or hives with frames and foundation or drawn comb.

6. Select frames containing brood, bees, and food stores from the original hive and place them in the new hive(s).

7. Ensure that each split has a queen or queen cells to ensure the development of a new queen.

8. Provide additional resources and manage the splits according to established beekeeping practices.

9. Hive splitting should be done carefully to avoid weakening the original colony and to ensure that each split has the necessary resources to develop into a viable colony.

Both capturing swarms and performing hive splits require experience, knowledge, and proper beekeeping equipment. It's important to have a good understanding of bee behavior, colony dynamics, and management techniques to successfully acquire bees through these methods. Consulting with experienced beekeepers or local beekeeping associations can provide valuable guidance and support when capturing swarms or performing hive splits.

Installing bees in the hive

Installing bees in the hive is an important step in starting a new colony or introducing bees to an existing hive.

Prepare the Hive:

1. Ensure that the hive is clean, assembled, and placed in its final location.

2. Remove any unnecessary equipment or debris from the hive.

3. Make sure the frames are inserted in the hive body and have foundation or comb for the bees to start building on.

Package Bees or Nuc Installation:

For Packaged Bees:

1. Spray the bees lightly with sugar water or plain water to help keep them calm.

2. Remove the top cover and any inner covers from the hive.

3. Carefully remove the queen cage from the package, being cautious not to damage her.

4. Create a space between the frames by pulling them apart slightly.

5. Gently pour or shake the bees into the hive, ensuring that most of them fall between the frames.

6. Place the queen cage, with the screen facing up, between the frames in the center of the hive.

7. Close the hive by placing the inner cover and top cover back in position.

For Nucleus Colonies (Nucs):

1. Remove the frames containing bees, brood, and resources from the nuc box.

2. Transfer the frames directly into the prepared hive, ensuring the frames are properly aligned.

3. Place the frames with brood in the center of the hive and arrange the remaining frames around them.

4. Check for the presence and placement of the queen in the nuc frames. If necessary, gently transfer her to the new hive.

5. Close the hive by placing the inner cover and top cover back in position.

Swarm Installation:

1. If you have captured a swarm or obtained one from another beekeeper, the process is slightly different.

2. Carefully transfer the swarm into the prepared hive, ensuring the queen is included.

3. Gently shake or brush the bees from the swarm container into the hive.

4. Allow the bees to settle inside the hive, ensuring that the queen is among them.

5. Close the hive by placing the inner cover and top cover back in position.

Provide Feed and Water:

1. After installing the bees, it's beneficial to provide them with a sugar syrup feeder to supplement their food supply, especially if nectar sources are limited.

2. Place a feeder filled with a sugar syrup mixture (1:1 ratio of water

and sugar) inside the hive. This helps the bees establish their colony and encourages comb building.

3. Ensure the bees have access to a nearby water source, such as a shallow dish or a waterer with rocks for them to land on.

Monitor and Assess:

1. Regularly monitor the hive to ensure that the bees are adjusting well, the queen is released (in the case of packaged bees), and the colony is developing properly.

2. Conduct regular inspections to check for signs of disease, pests, or any issues that may require attention.

3. Observe the bees' behavior and activity to ensure they are healthy and thriving.

Remember, specific installation techniques may vary depending on the package or nuc instructions, equipment used, and beekeeping practices in your region. It's recommended to consult with experienced beekeepers or local beekeeping associations for guidance specific to your area and beekeeping practices.

Regular hive inspections and maintenance

Regular hive inspections and maintenance are crucial for the health and productivity of your bee colony.

Inspection Frequency:

1. Conduct regular hive inspections based on the needs of your colony and the local beekeeping practices.

2. During the active season, when bees are actively foraging and building up their population, inspections may be conducted every 1-2 weeks.

3. In cooler months or during periods of minimal activity,

inspections can be less frequent, typically once a month or as necessary.

Safety Precautions:

1. Wear appropriate protective clothing, including a bee suit or jacket, veil, gloves, and closed-toe shoes to minimize the risk of bee stings.

2. Use a smoker to calm the bees before opening the hive. Puff some smoke near the hive entrance and around the top of the frames to encourage bees to move away.

Hive Inspection Process:

1. Begin by carefully removing the outer cover and inner cover of the hive.

2. Observe the bees' behavior at the hive entrance and look for any signs of abnormal activity or distress.

3. Inspect the frames one by one, starting from the outermost frame. Look for the presence of brood (eggs, larvae, and capped cells), pollen, honey stores, and signs of disease or pests.

4. Check for the presence and productivity of the queen. Look for eggs, larvae, and a healthy brood pattern.

5. Assess the overall health and population of the colony. Pay attention to the bees' behavior, their color, and any signs of disease or stress.

6. Take note of the amount of food stores available for the bees. Evaluate whether supplemental feeding is required.

7. Check for the presence of pests, such as varroa mites, and take appropriate measures for their management if necessary.

8. Make any necessary adjustments to the hive, such as adding or removing frames, adding supers for honey production, or providing additional space for the expanding colony.

Maintenance Tasks:

1. Ensure that the hive components are in good condition, including the hive bodies, frames, and foundation. Replace any damaged or deteriorated components.

2. Regularly clean the hive to remove debris, propolis, and excess beeswax.

3. Maintain proper ventilation in the hive by ensuring the entrance is clear and providing ventilation options if needed.

4. Monitor and manage honey supers, extracting honey when appropriate and adding additional supers as needed.

5. Address any issues or concerns identified during the inspection, such as signs of disease, pests, or overcrowding.

Record Keeping:

1. Keep detailed records of your hive inspections, noting the date, observations, and any actions taken.

2. This information helps you track the progress of your colony, identify patterns, and make informed management decisions.

Regular hive inspections and maintenance allow you to monitor the health of your bees, identify and address any issues promptly, and ensure the overall well-being of the colony. Consistency and attention to detail are key in maintaining healthy and productive beehives. Consulting with experienced beekeepers, attending workshops, or joining local beekeeping associations can provide valuable guidance and support in performing effective hive inspections and maintenance.

Checking for signs of disease and pests

When conducting hive inspections, it's essential to check for signs of disease and pests that can impact the health of your bee colony.

Varroa Mites:

1. Varroa mites are one of the most destructive pests for honeybee colonies.

2. Check for mites on adult bees, especially in the brood cells.

3. Look for deformed or damaged brood, including perforated cappings or pupae with mite-infested larvae.

4. Monitor mite levels using sticky boards or alcohol washes, following recommended methods.

5. Consider implementing integrated pest management (IPM) strategies to manage mite infestations.

American Foulbrood (AFB):

1. AFB is a highly contagious bacterial disease that affects bee broods.

2. Look for sunken, darkened, or perforated brood cappings.

3. Pay attention to foul or rotten odor emanating from the hive.

4. Discolored, slimy, and rope-like larvae are common signs.

5. If you suspect AFB, contact your local apiary inspector for proper diagnosis and guidance.

European Foulbrood (EFB):

1. EFB is another bacterial disease that affects bee broods.

2. Look for irregularly shaped, twisted, or discolored larvae.

3. Pay attention to uncapped or perforated brood cells.

4. Unlike AFB, larvae affected by EFB do not have the ropiness associated with AFB.

5. If EFB is suspected, seek guidance from a local beekeeping expert or apiary inspector.

Nosema:

1. Nosema is a fungal infection that affects the digestive system of bees.

2. Observe the behavior of adult bees. Increased defecation and dysentery may indicate Nosema infection.

3. Look for white or brown streaks on the outside of the hive, caused by infected bees defecating.

4. If Nosema is suspected, consult with a beekeeping expert to determine the appropriate treatment.

Small Hive Beetles (SHB):

1. SHBs are small, dark-colored beetles that infest beehives.

2. Check for adult beetles moving around in the hive, particularly in protected areas such as corners and crevices.

3. Look for larvae or pupae of the beetles in the frames or on the hive bottom.

4. Monitor the population of SHBs and implement control measures if necessary.

It's important to note that this is not an exhaustive list, and there are other diseases and pests that can affect honeybee colonies. Familiarize yourself with common diseases and pests in your region and consult with local beekeeping resources or experts for specific guidance and assistance in identifying and managing them. Regular monitoring and early detection are key to minimizing the impact of diseases and pests on your beehives.

Managing honey production and hive expansion

Managing honey production and hive expansion involves ensuring the availability of adequate resources for the bees, promoting a healthy and productive colony, and harvesting honey when appropriate.

Resource Availability:

1. Ensure the availability of sufficient nectar and pollen sources in the vicinity of the hive.

2. Provide a diverse range of flowering plants that bloom throughout the season to ensure a consistent food supply for the bees.

3. Avoid the use of pesticides and chemicals near the hive that may harm bees or contaminate honey.

Supering:

1. Supering involves adding additional hive boxes or supers to accommodate the expanding population and honey production.

2. Assess the strength of the colony and available resources before adding supers.

3. Place supers with foundation or drawn comb above the brood chamber to encourage bees to store surplus honey.

Honey Extraction:

1. Harvest honey when the frames are capped, and the honey has ripened sufficiently.

2. Use appropriate beekeeping tools, such as a honey extractor, to extract honey from the frames.

3. Follow proper hygiene practices during extraction to maintain the quality and cleanliness of the honey.

4. Leave sufficient honey stores for the bees to sustain themselves during periods of low nectar flow, such as winter.

Swarm Prevention:

1. Manage the colony's population to prevent swarming, which can reduce honey production and lead to the loss of bees.

2. Regularly inspect the hive for signs of overcrowding, such as the presence of queen cells or reduced space for brood and honey storage.

3. Perform hive splits or provide additional space for the expanding population to minimize the likelihood of swarming.

Queen Management:

1. Ensure the presence of a healthy and productive queen for optimal honey production.

2. Monitor the queen's performance by observing brood patterns, egg-laying activity, and the overall health and productivity of the colony.

3. Consider requeening if the queen is old, unproductive, or showing signs of poor performance.

Comb Management:

1. Replace old or damaged comb periodically to maintain hive hygiene and disease prevention.

2. Rotate frames and encourage bees to draw out new comb for brood and honey storage.

3. Monitor for signs of wax moth infestation or other issues that may affect the integrity of the comb.

Monitoring and Record Keeping:

1. Regularly monitor the hive's honey stores, brood development, and overall colony health.

2. Keep records of hive inspections, honey harvests, and other relevant observations to track the colony's progress and make informed management decisions.

It's important to note that honey production and hive expansion should be managed in alignment with the local climate, available forage, and the strength and needs of the colony. Consulting with experienced beekeepers or local beekeeping associations can provide valuable guidance tailored to your specific region and circumstances.

Feeding bees

Feeding bees becomes necessary in certain situations when natural nectar sources are limited or during periods of low food availability.

Insufficient Natural Food Sources:

1. In early spring or late fall, when there is limited flowering and nectar flow, bees may require supplemental feeding.

2. During drought conditions or in urban areas with limited floral resources, providing supplemental feed can ensure the bees have enough food.

New Colony Establishment:

1. When installing packaged bees or nucleus colonies (nucs) in a new hive, feeding them can help them establish and build up their stores.

2. Bees need to draw out comb and collect sufficient resources to sustain themselves, especially if there is a lack of natural forage.

Colony Expansion:

If you're actively managing the colony for growth and honey production, feeding can support their increased nutritional needs during periods of rapid population expansion.

Winter Preparation:

Before winter, it's crucial to ensure that the bees have enough honey stores to survive the colder months. If the colony's honey stores are insufficient, supplemental feeding with sugar syrup may be necessary to help them build up their winter reserves.

Considerations for Feeding Bees:

1. Sugar syrup is commonly used as a supplemental feed for bees. The most common ratio is a 1:1 mixture of granulated sugar and water (by weight) for stimulating brood production and colony growth.

2. For winter feeding, a 2:1 ratio (2 parts sugar to 1 part water, by weight) provides a higher concentration of sugar for longer-term storage.

3. Boil the water and dissolve the sugar completely. Allow the mixture to cool before providing it to the bees.

Feeder Types:

Choose appropriate feeders that minimize the risk of drowning or robbing by other bees.

Hive-top feeders, entrance feeders, or frame feeders are commonly used. Each has its advantages and considerations regarding ease of access, risk of spills, and potential for attracting pests.

Feeder Placement:

1. Place the feeder inside the hive, close to the brood area, for easy

access by the bees.

2. Ensure that the feeder does not cause congestion or block the normal movement of bees within the hive.

Monitoring:

Regularly monitor the food consumption and the bees' progress in building up their stores. Adjust feeding as necessary, ensuring a balance between providing enough food and allowing the bees to utilize natural forage when it becomes available.

Quality and Safety:

Use high-quality sugar without additives or contaminants. Ensure that all equipment used for feeding is clean and free from residues or chemicals that could harm the bees.

Remember, feeding bees should be approached as a temporary solution and should not replace the availability of natural forage whenever possible. Bees require a diverse and balanced diet for optimal health, so promoting and maintaining a healthy ecosystem with ample forage is essential for their overall well-being.

Chapter7: Beekeeping Challenges and Solutions

Common problems and pests

Beekeepers may encounter various problems and pests that can affect honeybee colonies. Here are some common issues to be aware of:

Varroa Mites:

Varroa mites are external parasites that attach themselves to honeybees and feed on their hemolymph (blood). They weaken the bees and transmit diseases. Regular monitoring and implementing integrated pest management (IPM) strategies are essential to manage varroa mite infestations effectively.

Small Hive Beetles (SHB):

SHBs are small, dark-colored beetles that lay eggs in beehives. The larvae then feed on honey, pollen, and bee brood, leading to damage and hive disruption. Keeping hives strong and well-maintained, maintaining proper hive ventilation, and using beetle traps can help control SHB populations.

Wax Moths:

Wax moths are pests that lay eggs in beehives, and their larvae feed on beeswax, honey, and brood comb. Weak or neglected colonies are particularly vulnerable. Maintaining strong colonies, regular hive inspections, and ensuring good hive ventilation can help prevent wax moth infestations.

Nosema:

Nosema is a fungal infection that affects the digestive system of bees, leading to reduced colony vigor and productivity. Proper hive hygiene, regular inspection for signs of infection, and maintaining a healthy environment can help prevent Nosema outbreaks.

American Foulbrood (AFB):

AFB is a highly contagious bacterial disease that affects bee broods. It is one of the most serious and destructive diseases for honeybee colonies. Regular inspection for AFB symptoms, practicing good hive management and hygiene, and prompt action in case of infection are crucial to prevent its spread.

European Foulbrood (EFB):

EFB is another bacterial disease that affects bee brood. Although less severe than AFB, it can still impact colony health and productivity. Maintaining strong and healthy colonies, providing a balanced diet, and practicing good hive management can help prevent EFB outbreaks.

Pesticide Exposure:

Bees can be exposed to harmful pesticides, which can cause adverse effects on their health and overall colony well-being. Educate yourself about pesticide usage in your area, communicate with local farmers or authorities about bee-friendly practices, and consider hive placement away from potential pesticide sources.

Queen Problems:

Queen issues, such as a failing or absent queen, can lead to decreased brood production, reduced colony strength, and overall hive decline. Regularly monitor the performance and presence of the queen, consider requeening if necessary, and ensure a healthy brood pattern.

Robbing:

Robbing occurs when bees from one colony invade and steal resources, such as honey, from another colony. It can lead to colony stress, disease transmission, and hive disruption. Prevent robbing by maintaining strong colonies, minimizing hive odors and spills, and using entrance reducers during periods of potential robbing.

Environmental Factors:

Environmental factors, such as extreme weather conditions, habitat loss, and pesticide exposure, can impact honeybee colonies' health and productivity. Maintain a diverse and pesticide-free forage environment, provide ample water sources, and consider local climate and habitat conditions when managing honeybee colonies.

Regular hive inspections, monitoring, and proactive hive management practices are crucial for detecting and addressing problems and pests early on. It's also essential to stay informed about local beekeeping practices and seek guidance from experienced beekeepers or local beekeeping associations for specific regional challenges and solutions.

Varroa mites and other parasites

Varroa mites are one of the most significant pests that honeybee colonies face. However, there are other parasites that can also affect bee health. Here's more information about Varroa mites and other common parasites:

Varroa Mites:

Varroa destructor is an external parasite that infests honeybee colonies worldwide. They attach to adult bees and brood, feeding on their hemolymph and transmitting diseases. Varroa mites weaken the bees' immune systems, shorten their lifespan, and can cause colony collapse if left untreated. Monitoring mite levels regularly and implementing effective control measures are crucial for colony health. Common control methods include using chemical treatments, integrated pest management (IPM) techniques, such as screen bottom boards and drone brood removal, and selective breeding for Varroa-resistant traits.

Tracheal Mites (Acarapis woodi):

Tracheal mites infest the tracheal tubes of honeybees, affecting their respiration and overall health. Infected bees may exhibit symptoms like shortened lifespan, reduced foraging capacity, and increased winter mortality. Monitoring and controlling tracheal mites can be challenging as they reside inside the bees' bodies. Methods for control include using menthol crystals, formic acid treatments, or specific miticides designed for tracheal mite control.

Nosema:

Nosema is a fungal parasite that affects the digestive systems of honeybees. The two common species are Nosema apis and Nosema ceranae. Infected bees may exhibit symptoms such as reduced colony vigor, increased defecation at the hive entrance, and dysentery. Proper hive hygiene, good nutrition, and stress reduction can help manage Nosema infections. Some treatments include using Fumagillin, a medication specifically designed to control Nosema, or essential oils with antimicrobial properties.

Small Hive Beetles (Aethina tumida):

Small Hive Beetles (SHB) are scavengers that lay eggs in beehives, and their larvae feed on honey, pollen, and bee brood. High SHB populations can cause damage to comb, ferment honey, and create conditions that lead to hive disruption. Controlling SHB involves maintaining strong colonies, providing good hive ventilation, and using beetle traps or oil traps to catch and remove the beetles.

Wax Moths (Galleria mellonella and Achroia grisella):

Wax moths lay eggs in beehives, and their larvae feed on beeswax, pollen, and honey. Weak or neglected colonies are more susceptible. Wax moth larvae can cause damage by tunneling through comb, leading to weakened hive structures. Maintaining strong colonies, good hive hygiene, and proper ventilation can help prevent wax moth infestations.

When managing honeybee colonies, it's important to regularly monitor for parasites, maintain strong and healthy colonies, and implement appropriate control measures when necessary. It's advisable to stay informed about the latest research and recommendations for parasite management and seek guidance from experienced beekeepers or local beekeeping associations for specific regional challenges and solutions.

Diseases and infections

Honeybee colonies can be susceptible to various diseases and infections. Here are some common ones to be aware of:

American Foulbrood (AFB):

AFB is a highly contagious and devastating bacterial disease caused by the spore-forming bacterium, Paenibacillus larvae. It affects the brood of honeybees, causing larvae to become dark, ropelike, and eventually disintegrate into a foul-smelling mass. AFB can lead to the death of the infected larvae and the collapse of the colony if left untreated. The primary method of control for AFB is the destruction of infected hives, followed by sanitation measures to prevent further spread. Antibiotics are not effective against AFB.

European Foulbrood (EFB):

EFB is another bacterial brood disease caused by Melissococcus plutonius. Infected larvae exhibit symptoms such as a twisted and discolored appearance, but they do not exhibit the ropiness seen in AFB. EFB can weaken colonies and impact their productivity. Control measures for EFB include improving colony health, requeening disease-resistant strains, and occasionally using antibiotics under veterinary guidance.

Chalkbrood:

Chalkbrood is a fungal disease caused by the fungus Ascosphaera apis. Infected larvae appear white and chalky, hence the name. Chalkbrood can weaken colonies, especially if there are large-scale infections. Good hive hygiene, reducing stress, and maintaining strong colonies can help manage chalkbrood. In severe cases, requeening or treatment with antifungal agents may be necessary.

Sacbrood Virus (SBV):

SBV is a viral disease that affects honey bee broods. Infected larvae exhibit symptoms such as a swollen appearance, giving them a sac-like appearance, before turning dark and rubbery. While SBV can weaken colonies, it usually does not cause colony death. Management techniques for SBV include maintaining strong colonies and requeening with hygienic or resistant stock.

Nosema:

Nosema is a fungal infection caused by Nosema apis and Nosema ceranae. Infected bees may exhibit symptoms such as dysentery, reduced lifespan, and decreased colony vigor. Good hive hygiene, reducing stress, and providing proper nutrition can help manage Nosema. Some treatments include using Fumagillin, an antibiotic specifically designed for Nosema control, or essential oils with antimicrobial properties.

Deformed Wing Virus (DWV):

DWV is a viral infection that affects honeybees, often in association with Varroa mite infestations. Infected bees exhibit deformed or shriveled wings, reduced flying ability, and overall weakness. Managing Varroa mite populations is essential in controlling DWV, as mites are known to vector the virus. Supporting colony health and reducing mite loads can help manage DWV.

Regular hive inspections, early detection of diseases, and implementing appropriate management strategies are crucial for maintaining healthy honeybee colonies. It's important to stay informed about the latest research and recommendations for disease management and seek guidance from experienced beekeepers or local beekeeping associations for specific regional challenges and solutions.

Swarm prevention and management

Swarm prevention and management are important aspects of beekeeping to maintain strong and productive colonies.

Provide Adequate Space:

Bees tend to swarm when they feel crowded in their hive. Ensure that the hive has enough space for the growing population, honey storage, and brood rearing. Regularly inspect the hive and add additional hive bodies (supers) or frames as needed to provide ample space.

Monitor Brood Nest Expansion:

Keep an eye on the brood nest expansion and honey storage in the hive. If the brood nest becomes congested or honey-bound (filled with honey and no space for the queen to lay eggs), consider redistributing frames or adding empty frames to provide more space.

Swarm Traps:

Set up swarm traps in strategic locations away from the main hive to capture swarms. Swarm traps can be baited with pheromones, such as a queen lure or lemon grass oil, to attract swarms.

Requeen:

Requeening the hive with a young and vigorous queen can help reduce swarming tendencies. Young queens tend to have higher egg-laying rates, which can prevent overcrowding and swarming impulses.

Splitting Hives:

Performing hive splits is a proactive method to manage swarming. By splitting a strong hive into two or more smaller colonies, you can alleviate overcrowding and give each colony space to grow.

Swarm Management Techniques:

If you notice signs of swarming, such as the presence of queen cells, take preventive action to manage the swarming impulse. Remove queen cells or perform a split to create a new colony. You can also perform a technique called "artificial swarm" by moving the original queen and a portion of the bees to a new hive, leaving the swarm cells behind in the original hive.

Monitor and Control Varroa Mite Levels:

High varroa mite infestations can increase the likelihood of swarming. Be sure to monitor and manage mite levels in the hive to keep them in check. Varroa mites weaken colonies and can contribute to the swarming impulse.

Provide Adequate Ventilation:

Proper hive ventilation helps regulate temperature and humidity in the hive, creating a comfortable environment for the bees. Good ventilation can help reduce stress and congestion, which may contribute to swarming.

Timely Harvesting of Honey:

Harvesting excess honey in a timely manner helps prevent the hive from becoming honey-bound, giving the bees more space to expand their brood nest.

Regular Hive Inspections:

Conduct regular hive inspections to monitor the colony's health, population size, and brood pattern. Early detection of swarm preparations, such as the presence of queen cells, can allow you to take timely action to prevent swarming.

Remember that swarm prevention and management are not foolproof, as swarming is a natural behavior of honeybees. However, implementing these strategies can help reduce the likelihood of swarming and provide opportunities to capture swarms or create new colonies.

Honey harvesting and processing

Honey harvesting and processing are exciting steps in beekeeping that allow you to enjoy the fruits of your bees' labor.

Timing:

Determine the appropriate time to harvest honey based on the nectar flow in your area and the readiness of the honey frames. Typically, honey is harvested in late spring or summer when there is abundant nectar available for bees to produce honey.

Tools and Equipment:

Ensure you have the necessary tools and equipment for honey harvesting, including a bee suit, gloves, a bee brush, a smoker, a hive tool, and a bee escape or fume board.

Preparing the Hive:

Before harvesting, ensure the bees have capped the honey cells. Capped cells indicate that the honey is ripe and ready for extraction. Remove any propolis or beeswax that may be blocking the honeycomb cells.

Honey Extraction:

Remove the frames containing capped honey from the hive. Brush off any bees on the frames using a bee brush or use a bee escape board to clear the bees from the frames before removing them. Place the frames in a bee-proof location to prevent being robbed by other bees.

Uncapping:

To extract honey, you need to uncap the honeycomb cells. This can be done using an uncapping knife, an electric uncapping knife, an uncapping fork, or an uncapping roller. Gently remove the wax cappings from both sides of the frame, exposing the honey.

Honey Extraction Methods:

There are various methods for extracting honey from the uncapped frames: Honey Extractor: Place the uncapped frames in a honey extractor, a device that uses centrifugal force to extract honey from the frames. Crush and Strain Method: Crush the uncapped frames and strain the crushed honeycomb through a fine mesh or cheesecloth to separate the honey from the wax and debris. Honey Press: Use a honey press to extract honey by pressing the honeycomb to release the honey.

Settling and Filtering:

After extraction, allow the honey to settle in a food-grade container for a day or two. This allows air bubbles and impurities to rise to the top. Filter the honey to remove any remaining wax, bee parts, or other debris. Use a fine mesh or a honey filter to achieve a clear and smooth final product.

Storage and Bottling:

Store the filtered honey in clean, dry, and airtight containers, such as glass jars or food-grade plastic bottles. Label the containers with the harvest date and any relevant information about the honey, such as the floral source or location. Store the honey in a cool, dry place away from direct sunlight to maintain its quality and prevent crystallization.

Remember to follow proper hygiene practices throughout the honey harvesting and processing process to ensure the quality and safety of your honey. Additionally, it's important to comply with local regulations and labeling requirements for selling or distributing honey.

If you're new to honey harvesting and processing, it's beneficial to seek guidance from experienced beekeepers or refer to comprehensive beekeeping resources for detailed instructions and best practices specific to your region.

Winter preparation and hive survival

Preparing your honeybee hives for winter is crucial to ensure the survival and well-being of your colonies during the colder months. Here are some important steps to consider for winter preparation:

Assess Hive Strength:

Evaluate the strength and population of each hive before winter. Strong colonies with sufficient numbers of bees are better equipped to survive winter. Combine weaker colonies if necessary to boost their chances of survival or consider requeening with a strong and healthy queen.

Varroa Mite Management:

Monitor and manage varroa mite populations in your hives. Varroa mites are a common threat to honeybees, and their presence can weaken colonies, making them more vulnerable during winter. Employ appropriate mite control measures, such as integrated pest management (IPM) techniques, including using approved treatments and methods to reduce mite infestations.

Feeding:

Ensure your bees have enough food stores to sustain them through the winter. Bees require sufficient honey or sugar syrup as their primary food source during winter when forage is limited. Conduct a thorough assessment of the honey stores in each hive. If necessary, provide supplemental feeding in the form of sugar syrup or fondant to bolster their food reserves.

Insulation and Ventilation:

Provide proper insulation to help regulate the temperature inside the hive. Insulating the outer cover, wrapping the hive with insulation material, or using insulation boards can help protect the bees from extreme cold. Ensure adequate ventilation in the hive to prevent excess moisture buildup, which can lead to condensation and mold growth. A top entrance or ventilation hole can help facilitate airflow.

Windbreaks and Shelter:

Shield the hives from harsh winds by placing them near natural windbreaks, such as trees, hedges, or fences. Consider using hive wraps or windbreaks made of burlap or other materials to provide additional protection against cold winds.

Reduce Hive Entrance:

Reduce the size of the hive entrance to a smaller opening using entrance reducers or mouse guards. This helps prevent cold drafts and intruders while allowing the bees to defend their hive.

Maintain Hive Hygiene:

Keep the hive clean and free of debris, dead bees, and excess moisture. Regularly inspect and remove any dead bees or debris from the bottom board and frames. Adequate hive hygiene helps create a healthier environment for the bees and reduces the risk of diseases and pests.

Monitor and Provide Emergency Feeding:

Throughout the winter, periodically check the hive's food reserves and overall health by listening for buzzing sounds or tapping the hive lightly to gauge the bees' response. If necessary, provide emergency feeding with fondant or candy boards if the bees' food stores are running low.

Continuous Monitoring:

Even during winter, it's important to monitor the hive periodically to ensure the bees' well-being. Check for signs of activity, condensation, or unusual sounds that might indicate issues requiring attention.

Remember that the specific winter preparation and management practices may vary depending on your geographical location and climate. It's always beneficial to consult with local experienced beekeepers or beekeeping associations to gain insights into region-specific techniques and recommendations for successful winter hive survival.

Chapter 8. Safety and Health Considerations

Understanding bee stings and allergic reactions

Bee stings are a common occurrence for beekeepers and can cause varying reactions, ranging from mild to severe. It's important to understand bee stings and allergic reactions to ensure your safety and take appropriate measures if needed.

Bee Sting Basics:

When a honeybee stings, it leaves behind its stinger, venom sac, and a small portion of its abdomen. The stinger continues to pump venom into the skin for a short time. Honey Bee stingers have barbs that can get lodged in the skin, causing the stinger to remain attached. It's important to remove the stinger promptly to minimize venom injection.

Mild Reactions:

Most people experience mild reactions to bee stings, which include pain, redness, swelling, and itching around the sting site. These symptoms usually subside within a few hours or a few days without the need for medical intervention.

Allergic Reactions:

Some individuals may have allergic reactions to bee stings, ranging from localized allergic reactions to severe systemic reactions. Localized Allergic Reactions: These reactions cause more pronounced swelling, redness, and itching that extend beyond the immediate sting site. They may last for a few days.

Systemic Allergic Reactions (Anaphylaxis): In rare cases, bee stings can trigger a severe allergic reaction known as anaphylaxis. Symptoms may include difficulty breathing, swelling of the face or throat, rapid heartbeat, dizziness, and loss of consciousness. Anaphylaxis requires immediate medical attention as it can be life-threatening.

Allergic Sensitization:

It's important to note that an allergic reaction to a bee sting can develop after repeated exposure. Initial stings may cause mild reactions, but subsequent stings can trigger more severe allergic responses. If you have experienced an allergic reaction to a bee sting in the past or have a known allergy to bee venom, it's essential to take extra precautions and consult with a healthcare professional.

Management and Prevention:

1. If you are stung by a bee, it's important to act promptly:

2. Remove the stinger as quickly as possible by scraping it out with a fingernail or using a flat, blunt object.

3. Wash the sting site with mild soap and water to prevent infection.

4. Apply a cold compress or ice pack to reduce swelling.

5. Over-the-counter antihistamines and pain relievers can help alleviate symptoms of mild reactions.

For individuals with known allergies or a history of severe reactions, carrying an epinephrine auto-injector (e.g., EpiPen) prescribed by a healthcare professional is essential in case of an anaphylactic reaction.

Seeking Medical Attention:

If you experience symptoms of anaphylaxis, such as difficulty breathing, throat swelling, or signs of a severe allergic reaction, seek immediate medical help. It's important to inform healthcare providers about any known allergies, previous reactions, or bee venom sensitization.

If you have concerns about bee stings or potential allergic reactions, it's advisable to consult with a healthcare professional or an allergist who can evaluate your specific situation, provide guidance, and prescribe appropriate medications or treatments if necessary.

Proper handling techniques to minimize stings

Bee stings can be minimized through proper handling techniques and precautions.

Wear Protective Clothing:

Always wear appropriate protective clothing when working with bees, including a bee suit or jacket, veil, and gloves. Ensure that your protective clothing fits well and covers all exposed areas of your body to prevent bees from reaching your skin.

Remain Calm and Gentle:

Bees are sensitive to sudden movements and vibrations. When working with bees, move slowly and avoid making sudden jerky movements that may irritate them. Handle the frames and hive components gently to avoid unnecessary disruption to the bees.

Use Smoke:

Smoke from a bee smoker helps calm the bees by interfering with their alarm pheromones and triggering them to consume honey, making them less defensive. Use the smoker sparingly, directing the smoke gently towards the entrance and the top of the hive. Avoid excessive smoke, which can harm the bees.

Work During Calm Weather:

Choose to work with your bees during calm weather conditions when bees are less likely to be agitated. Avoid working with the bees during rainy, windy, or extremely hot conditions, as it can make them more defensive.

Avoid Strong Fragrances:

Bees are attracted to strong fragrances, including scented lotions, perfumes, and hair products. Avoid using such products when working with bees. Additionally, avoid wearing bright-colored clothing, as bees are attracted to bright colors.

Be Mindful of Time:

Conduct hive inspections and other beekeeping activities during the day when most bees are out foraging. Working at night or during dusk can increase the chances of agitating the bees.

Proper Hive Manipulation:

Learn proper hive manipulation techniques to minimize disruption to the bees. Gently separate frames and avoid squishing or rolling bees between frames or hive components.

Know When to Stop:

Pay attention to the behavior of the bees during your interaction with them. If you notice increasing agitation or defensive behavior, it may be a sign to stop and close up the hive.

Learn Bee Behavior and Signals:

Observe and learn about bee behavior and signals to better understand their mood and reactions. Be aware of warning signs such as bees raising their abdomens or buzzing with increased intensity, indicating their defensive response.

Practice and Gain Experience:

With experience, you will become more comfortable and adept at working with bees, minimizing the risk of accidental stings. Regularly work with your bees to develop confidence and improve your beekeeping skills.

Remember, while these techniques can help minimize the risk of bee stings, it's essential to be prepared for the possibility of stings and know how to respond in case of an allergic reaction or emergency.

Using protective gear and maintaining hygiene

Using protective gear and maintaining hygiene are crucial practices to minimize the risk of bee stings and ensure your safety while working with bees.

Beekeeping Protective Gear:

1. Wear a bee suit or jacket made of lightweight, breathable material that covers your entire body. It should have elastic cuffs and ankle closures to prevent bees from entering.

2. Use a sturdy, well-fitting veil to protect your face and neck. Ensure the veil has good visibility and is securely attached to the suit or jacket.

3. Wear gloves made of thick, durable material that provide adequate protection while allowing for dexterity.

4. Consider wearing boots or shoes that cover your ankles and lower legs to protect against bee stings.

Maintaining Hygiene:

1. Keep your beekeeping gear clean and well-maintained. Regularly wash and sanitize your bee suit, veil, gloves, and other protective equipment.

2. Wash your hands thoroughly with soap and water before and after working with bees. This helps remove any lingering odors or substances that may attract or irritate bees.

3. Avoid using scented soaps, lotions, or other products with strong

fragrances that can attract bees.

Inspecting Protective Gear:

Before each use, carefully inspect your protective gear for any tears, holes, or other damage that could allow bees to enter. Repair or replace any damaged gear to ensure proper protection.

Proper Suit Closure:

Ensure that your bee suit or jacket is fully zipped up and closed, with no gaps or openings that bees can enter. Use Velcro straps or other closures to secure the suit tightly around your wrists and ankles. Check that the veil is securely attached to the suit or jacket, leaving no gaps for bees to enter.

Removing Stingers:

If you do get stung, promptly remove the stinger to minimize venom injection. Scrape the area gently with a flat object, such as a fingernail or hive tool, to dislodge the stinger. Avoid squeezing or pinching the stinger, as it can release more venom.

Cleaning Beekeeping Equipment:

Regularly clean and sanitize your beekeeping equipment, such as hive tools, frames, and honey extractors, to prevent the spread of diseases and pests among your colonies.

Storing Protective Gear:

Properly store your beekeeping gear in a clean and dry area, away from sunlight and potential contaminants. Hang or store your bee suit, veil, and gloves in a way that allows air circulation and prevents damage or mold growth.

Remember, while protective gear provides a physical barrier against bee stings, it's still important to practice gentle beekeeping techniques, stay calm, and be observant of bee behavior. Bees can be unpredictable, and it's crucial to prioritize your safety and take necessary precautions to minimize the risk of stings.

Chapter 9. Connecting with the Beekeeping Community

Participating in local beekeeping events

Participating in local beekeeping events can be a great way to enhance your knowledge, connect with fellow beekeepers, and stay updated with the latest practices in the field.

Local beekeeping events often feature workshops, seminars, and presentations by experienced beekeepers, researchers, and industry experts. These events provide valuable learning opportunities where you can acquire new skills, deepen your understanding of beekeeping techniques, and gain insights into beekeeping best practices.

Workshops may cover topics such as hive management, disease prevention, queen rearing, honey production, and more. Beekeeping events bring together beekeepers from your local community and beyond, allowing you to connect with like-minded individuals who share your passion for beekeeping.

Networking with other beekeepers can provide opportunities to exchange knowledge, share experiences, and seek advice on various aspects of beekeeping. Collaborative initiatives, such as joint honey extraction or swarm management, can be initiated through these networking connections.

Beekeeping events often feature exhibits by equipment manufacturers, suppliers, and beekeeping organizations. These exhibits provide an opportunity to explore and purchase beekeeping supplies, equipment, and tools that may not be readily available elsewhere. You can gather information about different beekeeping products, compare prices, and make informed decisions about your beekeeping needs.

Participating in local beekeeping events allows you to engage with your local community and raise awareness about the importance of bees and beekeeping. You can share your knowledge and experiences with attendees, answer questions, and promote bee-friendly practices in your area. Community engagement can help foster a positive image of beekeeping and contribute to the overall conservation and well-being of bees.

Some beekeeping events feature competitions and shows where beekeepers can showcase their honey, beeswax products, bee photography, or hive designs. Participating in these competitions can provide an opportunity to receive recognition for your efforts and achievements in beekeeping.

Check with your local beekeeping association or club for information about upcoming events in your area. Consult community event listings, agricultural fairs, or agricultural extension offices. Join online beekeeping forums or social media groups where members often share information about local events. Attending and participating in local beekeeping events can be both educational and enjoyable, offering you the chance to connect with fellow beekeepers, expand your knowledge, and contribute to the beekeeping community.

Networking with experienced beekeepers

Networking with experienced beekeepers can be highly beneficial for your beekeeping journey. Building connections with experienced beekeepers allows you to learn from their expertise, gain valuable insights, and receive guidance on various aspects of beekeeping.

Local beekeeping associations and clubs are excellent platforms to connect with experienced beekeepers in your area. Attend meetings, workshops, and events organized by these associations to meet and interact with seasoned beekeepers. Take advantage of the networking opportunities these gatherings offer to strike up conversations, ask questions, and build relationships.

Offer your assistance or inquire about apprenticeship opportunities with experienced beekeepers in your community. Volunteering or apprenticeship allows you to work alongside experienced beekeepers, observe their practices, and learn hands-on techniques. During your time together, ask questions, seek their advice, and express your eagerness to learn from their experience.

Beekeeping conferences and workshops attract beekeepers from different regions, including experienced individuals. These events provide opportunities to attend educational sessions, network with professionals, and engage in discussions on advanced beekeeping topics. Take advantage of networking breaks, social events, and panel discussions to connect with experienced beekeepers and exchange knowledge.

Participate in online beekeeping communities, forums, and social media groups dedicated to beekeeping. These platforms provide a virtual space to connect with beekeepers worldwide, including experienced individuals. Engage in discussions, ask questions, and seek advice from experienced beekeepers who actively participate in these communities.

Some experienced beekeepers may organize field days or offer opportunities to visit their apiaries. Keep an eye out for such events in your area and seize the chance to join them. These hands-on experiences allow you to witness beekeeping techniques firsthand and engage in conversations with the beekeeper.

Remember, when networking with experienced beekeepers, approach them with respect, gratitude, and a willingness to learn. Be prepared with specific questions or topics of interest to make the most of your interactions. Building relationships with experienced beekeepers takes time, so maintain a positive attitude, show genuine interest, and be open to their guidance and suggestions.

Sharing knowledge and experiences

Sharing knowledge and experiences with other beekeepers is a valuable way to contribute to the beekeeping community and foster a supportive learning environment. Here are some tips for effectively sharing your knowledge and experiences:

Join your local beekeeping association or club and actively participate in meetings, workshops, and events. Offer to share your experiences, insights, and tips during presentations or discussions. Be open to answering questions and providing guidance to fellow beekeepers based on your own experiences.

Join online beekeeping communities, forums, and social media groups where beekeepers gather to exchange information and seek advice. Share your knowledge and experiences by responding to questions, posting informative content, or starting discussions on relevant topics. Offer practical tips, troubleshooting advice, and lessons learned from your own beekeeping journey.

Consider starting a beekeeping blog or contributing articles to beekeeping publications or websites. Share your experiences, insights, and practical advice through well-written and informative posts. Discuss specific challenges you've encountered, solutions you've found, or techniques that have worked well for you.

Share your expertise by organizing workshops or training sessions for aspiring or beginner beekeepers. Teach practical beekeeping skills, demonstrate hive management techniques, or discuss specific topics of interest. Create a supportive learning environment where participants can benefit from their experiences and ask questions. Offer mentorship to beginner beekeepers who are starting their journey. Provide guidance, support, and encouragement as they navigate the challenges of beekeeping. Share your experiences, best practices, and lessons learned to help them avoid common pitfalls and build a strong foundation in beekeeping.

Consider participating in research projects or collaborating with researchers in the field of beekeeping. Share your observations, data, and experiences that can contribute to scientific understanding and the development of best practices. Publish your findings or experiences in beekeeping journals, magazines, or newsletters.

Remember, when sharing knowledge and experiences, be respectful, humble, and open-minded. Recognize that there are multiple approaches and perspectives in beekeeping and encourage healthy discussions and debates. Be willing to learn from others as well and embrace the spirit of collaboration and knowledge exchange within the beekeeping community.

Conclusion

In conclusion, beekeeping is a rewarding and fascinating hobby or profession that involves the management of honeybee colonies. By engaging in beekeeping, you contribute to the conservation of bees and their crucial role in pollination and ecosystem health. Throughout this guide, we have explored various aspects of beekeeping, including its benefits, the importance of bees in the ecosystem, acquiring knowledge and skills, hive components and tools, selecting bee species, hive placement, hive management, honey production, and dealing with challenges like pests and diseases.

Beekeeping requires dedication, ongoing learning, and responsible hive management. By joining local beekeeping associations, attending workshops, reading books, and connecting with experienced beekeepers, you can acquire the necessary knowledge and skills to be successful. Additionally, understanding local regulations, providing suitable hive locations, ensuring access to water and forage, and maintaining regular hive inspections are crucial for the well-being of your bees.

By actively participating in the beekeeping community, sharing knowledge, and learning from others, you contribute to the collective growth and success of beekeepers worldwide. Remember to prioritize safety by wearing appropriate protective gear, maintaining good hygiene, and seeking medical attention if necessary.

Embarking on a beekeeping journey is not only rewarding in terms of honey production but also in the joy of observing and supporting these incredible insects. Enjoy the process, embrace the learning opportunities, and savor the sweet rewards of beekeeping.